STUDIES ON INDUSTRIAL PRODUCTIVITY: SELECTED WORKS

Volume 3

VERTICAL INTEGRATION AND TECHNOLOGICAL INNOVATION

VERTICAL INTEGRATION AND TECHNOLOGICAL INNOVATION
A Transaction Cost Approach

YEONG HEOK LEE

Routledge
Taylor & Francis Group

LONDON AND NEW YORK

First published in 1994 by Garland Publishing Inc.

This edition first published in 2019
by Routledge
2 Park Square, Milton Park, Abingdon, Oxon OX14 4RN

and by Routledge
711 Third Avenue, New York, NY 10017

Routledge is an imprint of the Taylor & Francis Group, an informa business

British Library Cataloguing in Publication Data
A catalogue record for this book is available from the British Library

ISBN: 978-1-138-61548-9 (Set)
ISBN: 978-0-429-44077-9 (Set) (ebk)
ISBN: 978-1-138-31496-2 (Volume 3) (hbk)
ISBN: 978-1-138-31503-7 (Volume 3) (pbk)
ISBN: 978-0-429-45658-9 (Volume 3) (ebk)

Publisher's Note
The publisher has gone to great lengths to ensure the quality of this reprint but
points out that some imperfections in the original copies may be apparent.

Disclaimer
The publisher has made every effort to trace copyright holders and would welcome
correspondence from those they have been unable to trace.

VERTICAL INTEGRATION AND TECHNOLOGICAL INNOVATION

A TRANSACTION COST APPROACH

YEONG HEOK LEE

GARLAND PUBLISHING, Inc.
NEW YORK & LONDON / 1994

Library of Congress Cataloging-in-Publication Data

Lee, Yeong Heok, 1954–
    Vertical integration and technological innovation : a transaction cost
approach / Yeong Heok Lee.
        p.   cm. — (Garland studies on industrial productivity)
    Revision of thesis (Ph.D.)—Pennsylvania State University, 1988.
    Includes bibliographical references (p.   ).
    ISBN 0–8153–1569–4 (alk. paper)
    1. Vertical integration. 2. Efficiency, Industrial. 3. Transaction
costs. 4. Research, Industrial—Cost effectiveness. 5. Electronic
industries—United States—Vertical integration—Case studies. I. Title.
II. Series.
HD2748.L43   1994
338.5'1—dc20   93–38432
                                                        CIP

Printed on acid-free, 250-year-life paper
Manufactured in the United States of America

CONTENTS

Page

LIST OF TABLES ix

LIST OF FIGURES xi

ACKNOWLEDGEMENTS xii

Chapter

1 INTRODUCTION 3

   1.1 Research Motivation 3
   1.2 Research Overview 5

2 COSTS AND BENEFITS OF VERTICAL
   INTEGRATION 8

   2.1 Transaction Cost Approach to Vertical
      Integration 8

      2.1.1 Various Rationales for Vertical
           Integration 8
      2.1.2 Transaction Cost Approach to Vertical
           Integration 9

   2.2 Cost-Benefit Analysis of Vertical
      Integration 12
   2.3 Summary 16

Chapter   Page

3   KNOWLEDGE COMPLEMENTARITY EFFECT
    AND TRANSACTION COSTS 19

    3.1 Knowledge Complementarity Effect of
         Vertical Integration 19

         3.1.1 The New Institutions for Technological
                Innovation....................................... 19
         3.1.2 The Modes of Knowledge
                Complementarity 22
         3.1.3 Free Communication and the Employment
                Relationship.................................... 27

    3.2 Transaction Costs of Technology
         Transaction 31

         3.2.1 Asymmetric Information in Technology
                Transaction 31
         3.2.2 Human Capital and Opportunism 34
         3.2.3 Integration and Technology Leakages ... 36

    3.3 Summary 38

Chapter   Page

4   VERTICAL INTEGRATION AND TECHNOLOGICAL
    INNOVATION IN THE U.S. ELECTRONICS
    INDUSTRY 42

    4.1 Introduction 42
    4.2 The Sample 47
    4.3 The Variables 52
    4.4 Estimating the Equation of Knowledge
        Production 68

        4.4.1 Patents as a Dependent Variable 70
        4.4.2 R & D Expenditure (R&D) as a Dependent
              Variable 78
        4.4.3 R & D Intensity (RND) as a Dependent
              Variable 83

    4.5 Estimating the Equation of Vertical
        Integration 85
    4.6 Summary, Limitations, and Suggested Further
        Research 98

5   CONCLUSION 104

Chapter   Page

BIBLIOGRAPHY 106

Appendix A: **THE DISTRIBUTION OF PATENTS
APPLIED FOR BY DATE GRANTED:
1970-1977** 115

Appendix B: **ESTIMATING VI EQUATION WITH
ADDITIVE SUM OF VARIABLE FI** 116

LIST OF TABLES

Page

1. Costs and Benefits of "Make or Buy" Decisions 14

2. Technology Development and Acquisition
   Methods 21

3. The List of Sample Companies 52

4. The Variables and Their Expected Signs 63

5. Means of Firm-Level Variables by Year,
   1966-1986 65

6. Means of Firm-level Variables by Firm 66

7. Means and Pearson Product Moment Correlation
   Coefficients 67

8. OLS Regression Model 1 75

9. OLS Regression Model 2 76

10. OLS Regression Model 3 77

11. OLS Regression Model 4 80

12. OLS Regression Model 5 81

13. OLS Regression Model 6 82

Page

14. OLS Regression Model 7 86

15. OLS Regression Model 8 87

16. 2SLS Regression Models 94

17. SYSNLIN OLS Regression 1 95

18. SYSNLIN OLS Regression 2 96

LIST OF FIGURES

Page

1. The Modes of Knowledge Complementarity 26

2. The Stable and Unstable Conditions 45

3. The Bias and Inconsistency of OLS Estimates 46

ACKNOWLEDGEMENTS

This book is a revised version of my doctoral dissertation, defended at The Pennsylvania State University, University Park, Pennsylvania, in June 1988. I would like to express my deepest appreciation to Dr. Keith J. Crocker, thesis advisor, who provided considerable guidance and encouragement through his great personality. This book would not have been possible without his urging and support. I would like to extend the thanks to the other members of my doctoral committee, Dr. Irwin Feller (chair of committee), Dr. Mark Roberts, and Dr. Gary Lilien, for their helpful comments and suggestions on the expositions and the empirical work.

I am grateful to Dr. Shagil Ahmed who gave me a good knowledge on the nonlinear estimation technique. I would like to thank Dr. Kang Rae Cho who always encouraged me and provided good ideas on writing this thesis. And I appreciate the help of Dr. Bum Ha Jee and Dr. Sang Youl Kim for the computer work and drawing figures.

I appreciate The Korea Institute for Economics and Technology (KIET) for valuable financial support during the early years of my graduate study in Penn State.

Finally, I want to give all my love and special thanks to my wife, Young Mi, and daughters, Ji Sun and Ji Yoon, for their support, patience, and encouragement.

Vertical Integration
and Technological
Innovation

I
Introduction

1.1 RESEARCH MOTIVATION

The purpose of this study is to investigate the relationship between a firm's decision to integrate vertically and its research and development (R & D) strategy. As a modern economy grows and technology develops rapidly, technological competition between rival firms has become more severe. While there are many different means by which a firm to obtain a technological advantage, one of the more important ways is how it reorganizes itself to conduct or absorb technological knowledge. One of these means is vertical integration.

Vertical integration changes not only the number of products produced by a firm, but also involves changes in all the resources of a firm such as human resources, manufacturing facilities, and stock of technological endowment, and changes in their functions within a firm. A firm's decision to integrate vertically may not depend on any instant and short-term beneficial effects or cost savings. Rather the managerial decision for vertical integration may represent a comprehensive and future-oriented strategy designed to improve the firm's global environment for future progress. This view of vertical integration as a long-term management strategy leads to an examination of its relation to research and development activity, because R & D is more frequently characterized by uncertainty and a longer-range objective. The strategic coincidence of vertical integration and technological innovation is implied by the following remark from Friar and Horwitch (1985):

Technology strategy has intimate ties with

3

the other functional strategies of a corporation, including marketing, manufacturing, finance, and human resources. Moreover, it has a profound impact on the business strategies of a firm, such as in creating synergies between businesses, in extending or transforming the life cycles of various products, or in creating opportunities for forward and backward vertical integration. (p. 145)

Unfortunately this insight has not been considered in most of the literature on vertical integration.[1] Thus, we are motivated to investigate whether or not vertical integration is related to R & D activity. In this research, we ask two basic questions: (1) is vertically integrated firm structure a "good" environment to increase the productivity of R & D activity? and (2) does the firm that expects to have more future innovation integrate vertically more so than other firms? Therefore, the tasks of our study are to combine two different fields of economics -- vertical integration and technological innovation; to relate them; and to examine any possible simultaneous feedback effect between them.

The theory of vertical integration[2] has been studied in the context of the theory of the firm. After Coase (1937) defined the difference between a firm and a market in terms of transaction costs, Williamson (1975) set up the basic theory of transaction cost economics. The transaction cost approach to vertical integration is used in this paper, since transaction cost can explain many rationales for vertical integration.

While the relationship between market structure and innovation has been a common research topic in the study of technological innovation, the study of the firm-specific effects of technological innovation -- which is the study of environmental firm-specific effects inside the black box of R & D activity -- is still at a formative stage. The traditional argument concerning the relationship between market structure and a firm's R & D activity centers on the scale economies in R & D. According to the "Schumpeterian hypothesis," a larger firm's R & D activity is more intensive than a smaller firm's because the larger firm's R & D generates a greater return than the smaller firm's. That is, because they expect that the productivity per dollar of research expenditure will increase as size grows, such firms will devote more resources to R & D compared to their sizes. While a lot of work has been done in this field, there remains a considerable debate over the empirical evidence to support this view.[3]

In this dissertation we propose that the vertical integration, rather than the size of a firm, generates a greater return on the firm's R & D through what we term the "knowledge complementarity" effect. In addition, we hypothesize that a firm decides to vertically integrate because such integration can mitigate the market transaction costs associated with expected future innovation. The reason why the firm does not use the external market for its future innovation, namely why the firm emphasizes internal R & D through vertical integration rather than uses technology licensing or R & D contracting, will be explained in a transaction cost context.

1.2   RESEARCH OVERVIEW

After the introduction (chapter 1), we review the literature on vertical integration and present a framework to analyze the costs and benefits of vertical integration in chapter 2. In chapter 3 we investigate the theoretical basis for our main hypotheses, and in chapter 4 we test the hypotheses empirically.

As we develop our arguments in the context of transaction cost economics, we adopt the basic concept that no externality effect exists in the strict sense. This concept means that all externalities would be eliminated by bargaining, while the bargaining accompanies transaction costs. This is because the existence of externalities implies that bargains could be made that would improve the welfare of all concerned, as Warren-Boulton (1978) indicated. The notion that the same effect with externalities can be obtained through bargaining in the external market will be the starting point for our cost-benefit analysis of vertical integration.

The two basic tools necessary to relate vertical integration and technological innovation are the knowledge complementarity effect[4] and transaction costs. Knowledge complementarity explains the mechanism by which vertical integration helps innovative activity, and transaction costs explain the reason why vertical integration, rather than the external market, is used for efficient future innovation.

The terminology of "knowledge complementarity effect" represents "informational economies" in knowledge production. The knowledge complementarity effect of vertical integration means that upstream and downstream production processes within a firm use some common knowledge and provide relevant information to help one another become more efficient in R & D. Transaction costs are the costs of organizing economic activity, not the costs of producing real products. The transaction costs of technology licensing or R & D contracting occur due to the information asymmetry problem in technology-related transactions. Technology buyers necessarily know less about the technology than the sellers, because the information about the technology is the product itself. Chapter 3 develops these two concepts in detail.

Chapter 4 presents empirical evidence for the arguments addressed in the initial chapters. The evidence is based on a study of vertical integration and technological innovation in the U.S. electronics industry. The empirical test featuring the assumptions and technique of the rational expectations hypothesis uses a dynamic simultaneous equation model with expectation variables and various time lags.

Concluding remarks appear in chapter 5 along with some suggestions for future research.

Notes

1. An exception is Armour and Teece (1980) who argued that the more vertically integrated firm would be more efficient in R & D than the less vertically integrated firm. But they did not explain the strategic coincidence or simultaneity effect between vertical integration and R & D strategy.

2. Vertical integration means the extent to which a firm carries on the production processes from raw materials to final product in itself. The terminology of vertical integration should be used differently from the behaviour like vertical merger. Vertical integration is achieved through vertically merging another firm or building new input-producing plant.

3. Scherer's review of the empirical evidence pointed to a threshold effect: up to a certain level of size, the larger firm's R & D generates a greater return than the smaller firm's, but beyond that level further bigness added little or no increase on the rate of return (Scherer, 1980, p. 422).

4. We use knowledge interchangeably with information in this study, while knowledge is the contents and information refers to the process of knowledge transfer. Since knowledge is a valuable product to be transacted in the market, We exclude the notion of negative knowledge. According to Machlup (1980), the members of the negative knowledge set are erroneous knowledge, contradicted knowledge, obsolete knowledge, rejected knowledge, questionable knowledge, uncertain knowledge, vague knowledge, illusive knowledge, confusing knowledge, and so on.

II
Costs and Benefits of Vertical Integration

2.1 TRANSACTION COST APPROACH TO VERTICAL INTEGRATION

2.1.1 Various Rationales for Vertical Integration

Most of the literature on vertical integration to date has focused mainly on two sets of motives: market power and efficiency. In market power considerations, the purpose of a firm's vertical integration was either to gain extra profit through price discrimination, or to forestall entry through market foreclosure or denial of material supply. Perry (1980) found that forward integration by Alcoa was done mainly for the purpose of price discrimination. Crandall (1968) explained the backward integration of motor vehicle producers with price discrimination and market foreclosure. Allen (1971) examined the market foreclosure complaint against the vertical integration of a cement company and a producer of ready-mixed concrete. While the courts have raised several objections to vertical integration based upon antitrust law, most economists could not find much support for the notion that vertical integration was generally used for anticompetitive purposes. In order for the integrating firm to succeed in price discrimination or to forestall entry through vertical integration, the integrated firm must already have had some market power in its product market.

While market power considerations do not sufficiently explain vertical integration, efficiency considerations have received a great deal of attention from economists. The most popular explanation concerned economies of scope between successive stages due to technological and organizational interrelationships (Bain, 1959; Chandler, 1966).[1] Other arguments have dealt with the avoidance of factor distortions in a downstream firm's production when monopolistic input supply is integrated to a downstream production process (Vernon and Graham, 1971; Warren-Boulton, 1974); a downstream firm's information acquisition about the uncertainty of an upstream goods' supply (Arrow, 1975); the transfer of uncertainty from a downstream firm to an upstream firm (Carlton, 1979); and the avoidance of demand variability (Bernhardt, 1977). Furthermore, it has been pointed out that transaction costs might create important incentives for vertical integration (Coase, 1937; Williamson, 1975). Recently, many economists have emphasized transaction costs as a rationale for vertical integration and have tested them empirically (Monteverde and Teece, 1982; Mowery, 1983; Anderson and Schmittlein, 1984; Masten, 1984; Levy, 1985). We will develop our hypothesis on efficiency considerations, which is centered on the transaction cost argument.

2.1.2 Transaction Cost Approach to Vertical Integration

The theory of transaction cost economics goes back to the era of Coase(1937). When he answered "why a firm emerges at all in a specialized exchange economy," he cited transaction costs as the reason. He identified a transaction cost as "a cost of using the price mechanism"(p. 390). The costs of organizing production through the price mechanism are those stemming from the discovery of what the relevant prices are; from negotiating and concluding a contract; from a lack of flexibility associated with long-term contracts; and from a sales tax on market transactions. After he mentioned the cost of transacting within a firm (internalization cost) as "diminishing returns to management," Coase summarized the reason for a firm's emergence in one paragraph:

> A firm will tend to expand until the costs of
> organizing an extra transaction within the
> firm become equal to the costs of carrying
> out the same transaction by means of an
> exchange on the open market or the costs
> of organizing in another firm. (p. 395)

Since then, this remark has been the subject of all the transaction cost studies. We will also develop our arguments within this boundary.

In his famous book, *Markets and Hierarchies* (1975), Williamson located the sources of transaction costs in the characteristics of human nature. These characteristics are labeled "bounded rationality" and "opportunism." Bounded rationality refers to the limited ability of a rational human to receive, store, and process information. Because of this limit, uncertainty may exist at the individual level when all relevant data are theoretically available, that is, when no market uncertainty is present (Blair and Kaserman, 1983, p. 20). Opportunism implies a type of behavior in which individuals attempt to realize gains "through a lack of candor or honesty in transactions" (Williamson, 1973, p. 317), and "seek self-interest with guile" (Williamson, 1985, p. 47). More generally, opportunism refers to the incomplete or distorted disclosure of information, especially to calculated efforts to mislead, distort, disguise, obfuscate, or otherwise confuse (Williamson, 1985, p. 47).

Besides these human factors, Williamson identified market uncertainty and asset specificity as the environmental factors which increase the costs of market exchange. Market uncertainty refers to the unpredictable change of price, quality, supply, or demand for the intermediate product. Uncertainty arises from random acts of nature, unpredictable changes in consumer preferences, and lack of communication (Williamson, 1985, p. 57). As the degree of uncertainty increases, the contracts will be more lengthy and complex. Asset specificity, which is a common source of "the small numbers bargaining problem," arises when traders' options for transferring their businesses to alternative suppliers or buyers are limited (Blair and

Kaserman, 1983, p. 19). This is a "lock in" effect due to "(1) specific investments made by the winner of the original contract or (2) the creation of firm-specific human capital as a result of carrying out the terms of the original contract" (p. 19). Asset specificity causes opportunism to become particularly acute in the contract renewal. Besides these four factors, Williamson (1975) introduces another concept of "information impactedness" which is a derivative condition that arises mainly because of uncertainty and opportunism. Information impactedness means a circumstance where private information about a transaction is exploited for opportunistic behaviour.

The above four factors (opportunism, bounded rationality, uncertainty, and asset specificity) are the source of transaction costs. As the choice of an institutional alternative depends on the minimizing of transaction costs, these factors will be the important determinants of vertical integration. While most writers argue that transaction cost considerations underlie all the prominent reasons for vertical integration, such as the elimination of monopoly distortions, technical complementarities, supply reliability and economies in the acquisition of information, they came short of explaining the transaction costs of technology licensing or R & D contracting as an underlying reason for vertical integration. This technology-related transaction cost is especially important in explaining the vertical integration of today's high-tech industry.[2]

In arguing that technological interdependency between successive stages of a production process is not good enough to explain vertical integration, Williamson says that transaction costs are what explains the decision to integrate (1975, ch. 5). He believes that because technological complementarity can be accomplished through external market transactions as well as through internalization, there should be an additional explanation as to why firms choose internalization for technological complementarity. The explanation lies in the transaction cost related to external market transactions for technological complementarity.

2.2 Cost-Benefit Analysis of Vertical Integration

In this section we will examine the costs and benefits involved in a firm's "make" decision and "buy" decision in order to explain the costs and benefits of vertical integration in a transaction-cost framework. The "make or buy" decision of a component is basically the same as a firm's decision to integrate vertically, since the internal production of each component results in the change of the extent of a firm's vertical production processes. We concentrate on knowledge complementarity effect (i.e., informational economies) as a benefit of the "make" decision and on its relevant transaction cost as a cost of the "buy" decision. We argue that vertical integration provides a good environment for R & D activity through the knowledge complementarity effect; thus, the desire to enhance future innovation becomes an important determinant of vertical integration. We also argue that the transaction cost related to the externality effect of knowledge complementarity, which means the transaction cost of either buying the needed technology later in the external market (technology licensing) or using an external market contract to get the needed knowledge service during the R & D activity (R & D contracting), will be large compared to the transaction cost related to the externality effect of technical or physical complementarity. In other words, we hypothesize that the cost of transacting mental power is greater than the cost of transacting physical power. This is because of the information asymmetry problem and the opportunistic behavior of individual agents in a technology transaction, which will be explained later.

The traditional approach in a "make or buy" decision was to compare the internal and external costs needed for a given fixed benefit. For example, Coase says that, "the costs of organizing an extra transaction within the firm are equal to the costs involved in carrying out the transaction in the open market (in an equilibrium state)" (1937, p. 394). Following this, most empirical work on "make or buy" decisions with transaction cost argument compared the transaction cost and the internalization cost of a given component by examining the transactional characteristics of the component (e.g., Monteverde and Teece, 1982; Masten, 1984). In this study, besides the transaction and internalization costs of the component itself, we will include the externality effects of the component's internal production and its relevant transaction costs in the scheme of cost-benefit analysis for a firm's "make or buy" decision.

Before we proceed, we need to differentiate transaction costs from production costs. According to Arrow (1971),

> The distinction between transaction costs and production costs is that the former can be varied by a change in the mode of resource allocation, while the latter only depend on the technology and tastes, and would be the same in all economic systems. (p. 68)

In our cost-benefit analysis we assume that production cost is the same in all economic systems; thus, we are concerned about only transaction costs.

In Table 1, each "make" and "buy" decision has its own benefit and cost. Benefit U is the utility which a firm obtains from using a component. Therefore, it is the same in both the "make" and the "buy" decision. Cost T is the transaction cost in buying the component through a market exchange, and cost C is the internalization cost of organizing additional transactions within the firm to produce it internally. UI stands for such additional benefits of internal production (externalities) as informational and physical complementarity effect, avoidance of factor distortion, and demand and supply reliability. ΔU stands for the benefits in UI that can be obtained through relevant contracts in the market. The examples of the relevant contracts will be common usage of tools, co-location of plants, long-term

Table 1: Costs and Benefits of "Make or Buy" Decisions

	Buy	Make
Benefit	$U + \Delta U$	$U + UI$
Cost	$T + \Delta T_1 + \Delta T_2$	C

supply of components, and mutual knowledge service for R & D activity. But in order to earn the benefits ΔU from these external market contracts, a firm has to incur the transaction costs of ΔT_1 and ΔT_2. ΔT_1 is the explicit transaction cost of writing the complex contracts that would be required to obtain ΔU. ΔT_2 is the endogenous transaction cost, which refers to the economic inefficiency in non-Pareto optimal production of the component and the final good due to the private information holder's opportunistic behavior (Crocker, 1982).[3] ΔU from the external market is intrinsically smaller than the UI of the internal production. Only an infinite number of contracts and enforcement will bring ΔU close to UI in the limit. That is, $\lim_{\Delta T \to \infty} \Delta U = UI$. This explains the limit of the contractual relationship in producing the additional benefits UI of internal production, a limit which is due to imperfect knowledge and opportunistic behavior. A firm will review the benefit and cost of using external market and internal market at the time of the "make or buy" decision. Masten (1984) compared T and C, and Levy (1985) compared UI, T and C without considering ΔU and ΔT (ΔT_1 and ΔT_2). Our analysis will show that ΔU and the transaction costs ΔT involved in obtaining ΔU from the external market are very important in a "make or buy" decision.

For example, if a steel firm buys cold iron from an

iron firm, it will get the benefit of U and be liable for the transaction cost T involved in the market transaction of cold iron, which is probably fairly small in this case. If a steel firm internalizes the production of iron, it will get the benefit of U + UI (where UI is thermal economies) and bear the internalization cost of C involved in organizing iron production within the firm. In this case, the firm will need to compare only T, C and UI in a "make or buy" decision.

Alternatively, suppose that this steel firm wants to buy hot iron in the external market to obtain some of the thermal economies, ΔU. It will then need to make additional contracts with the iron producer for such things as the co-location of steel and iron plants. These additional contracts bring about additional explicit transaction cost (contractual cost ΔT_1) relative to cold iron and lead to opportunistic behavior due to their asset specificity (endogenous transaction cost ΔT_2). Therefore, in this case the firm will need to consider how much transaction cost ΔT is needed for any ΔU as well as T, C, and UI in the "make or buy" decision. Like the above example of technical complementarities (thermal economies), firms can get any of the additional benefits of supply reliability, knowledge complementarity, and elimination of monopoly distortion through additional contracts, while incurring the transaction cost ΔT. That is, the externality effects resulting from internalization should be obtainable through bargaining between all those concerned in the external market.

As another example, besides buying semi-conductors, if a computer firm buys technology service from a semi-conductor firm in order to develop a new model of a computer (R & D contracting), it will incur an additional transaction cost ΔT. The transaction cost ΔT in technology transaction for knowledge complementarity is assumed to be larger than the transaction cost ΔT in the transaction for physical or technical complementarity, which implies the relevancy of future innovation as a determinant of vertical integration. This is because of the particular phenomenon of the asymmetric information problem and opportunism due to the involvement of human capital in technology transaction which will be explained in the next chapter. That is, in a market characterized by uncertainty such as a technology-related market, externalities abound. And the endeavor to obtain the externality through relevant contracts in the external market will bring about big transaction costs.

In summary, because UI > ΔU and ΔT_1, ΔT_2 > 0, the bigger the UI (externality effect) the internalization acquires and the larger the ΔT (additional transaction costs related to ΔU) the "buy" decision causes, the more favorable the "make" decision is. Therefore, our first hypothesis is that vertical integration produces a greater return on R & D through knowledge complementarity. The second hypothesis is that the more a firm expects to have future innovation, the more it expects to be involved in a technology transaction that brings about big transaction costs. And thus our empirical work will test whether a firm which expects significant future innovation will vertically integrate more than others.

2.3 SUMMARY

In this chapter we surveyed various rationales for vertical integration. After reviewing the transaction cost approach to vertical integration in detail, we devised a scheme for analyzing the costs and benefits of vertical integration.

Among the various efficiency purposes of vertical integration, the knowledge complementarity effect was emphasized as an important one. After addressing that transaction costs accompany any endeavor to obtain the efficiency effects (externalities) in the external market, we hypothesized that the transaction cost of knowledge complementarity would be larger than the transaction cost of physical complementarity.

In our analytic framework, efficiency effects, transaction costs, and internalization costs were the determinants of vertical integration. Our model includes (1) knowledge complementarity and demand reliability as the variables for efficiency effects, (2) their relevant transaction costs, (3) managerial efficiency as the variable for internalization costs, and (4) asset specificity as the variable for the initial transaction costs.

Notes

1. A formal example is thermal economies of producing iron and steel at the same site.

2. Although no strict definitions are available, high technology industries are characterized by rapid technological change and a high proportion of engineers and scientists to total employment (Cremeans et al., 1984, p. 39). Some examples of high-tech industries are plastic materials and synthetic rubber, drugs, computing and office equipment, communication equipment, electronic components and accessories, aerospace, measuring and controlling instruments, and so on (ibid., p. 41).

3. When there are many sellers for a homogeneous product, there is no room for a firm to exploit its private information opportunistically. When there is an informational disadvantage for a buyer, the products are never homogeneous from the perspective of the buyer. In this case, increasing the number of asymmetrically informed sellers does not result in a dimunition of the "information rents" (see Akerlof [1969] and Rothschild and Stiglitz [1976]).

III
Knowledge Complementarity Effect
and
Transaction Costs

The terminology of "knowledge complementarity effect" means "informational economies" in knowledge production. In the first half of this chapter we will look into the mechanisms inside the black box of innovative activity and see how vertical integration technologically provides a better environment for R & D. In the second half of this chapter we will explain the economic reason for the choice of vertical integration over external sources in the firms' expected future innovations. The reason stems from the transaction costs of technology trading.

3.1 KNOWLEDGE COMPLEMENTARITY EFFECT OF VERTICAL INTEGRATION

3.1.1 The New Institutions for Technological Innovation

Technology has emerged recently as an essential part of corporate strategy. Firms which put great strategic emphasis on technological innovation are using several methods for technology development and acquisition. Among the methods identified in Table 2, the internal methods refer to the R & D activity inside the firm. The external methods relate to the way technologies are acquired in the external market either by contract or by purchase. But in our study, the methods, such as external acquisition of another firm for the purpose of technology acquisition, should be differentiated from the technology-purchasing method of contracting or licensing although both of them are called external methods, because the former methods change the firm's size and structure. An example of the former method is the vertical merger of another firm for the purpose of technology acquisition. Vertical merger, which changes the firm's manufacturing capacity, its range of produced products, and number of R & D personnel, is presented as a way of fostering the rate of return on future R & D rather than a way of acquiring the technology itself.

According to M. N. Friedman (1958), about 250 of the 2,000 corporate mergers and acquisitions in mining and manufacturing industries during the five-year period from 1952 through 1956, were reported to have occurred due to research and development considerations.[1] Friedman (1958) provides a rationale for a R & D-related merger:

> The acquiring company may wish to obtain
> an established patent base in the new field
> it is entering. Even where such a base is
> obtainable by licensing, the company may
> prefer for competitive reasons to exercise
> direct control over the patents involved.
> (p. 34)

Friedman draws his rationale simply from "competitive reasons," which mean advantages in terms of more extensive, effective, and diversified future R & D. Although he points out that effective product diversification or future innovation is an important rationale for merger or acquisition, he can not explain why merger or acquisition is more effective than licensing in future innovation and diversification. In this study, we will explain the rationales for vertically related mergers or acquisitions both through knowledge complementarity effect and in terms of the associated transaction cost considerations. In this chapter we will define the knowledge complementarity effect and show how it is achieved in the vertically related firm.

Table 2: Technology Development and Acquisition Methods

Internal

1. Technologies developed originally in the central R & D lab or division
2. Technologies developed using internal venturing, entrepreneurial subsidiaries, independent business units,etc.

External

3. Technologies developed through external contracted research
4. External acquisition of firms primarily for technology-acquisition purposes
5. As a licensee for another firm's technology
6. Joint ventures to develop technology
7. Equity participation in another firm to acquire or monitor technology

Source: Friar and Horwitch (1985, p. 166), originally from E. B. Roberts, "New Ventures for Corporate Growth," *Harvard Business Review*, (July-August, 1980).

Knowledge complementarity is an element of UI in Table 1 if the complementarity is obtained through internalization. It corresponds to an element of ΔU if it is achieved through the external market. The terminology of knowledge complementarity as a rationale for vertical integration has not been used in the economic literature. Instead, the literature has referred to "informational economies or economies of information exchange" (Williamson, 1971), or "efficiency of vertical integration in technological similarities and complementarities" (Armour and Teece, 1980). In this study, we will use "knowledge complementarity" rather than "technological complementarity," in order to emphasize knowledge complementarity rather than such physical complementarities as thermal economies and the usage of common tools. This terminology is more appropriate than "informational economies" when explaining the mechanisms of interdependency of upstream and downstream R & D and interdependency of R & D division and production division.

Knowledge complementarity between different producers and users recently has been stressed by a number of R & D decision makers in government, corporate, and academic environments. This is reflected in the recent emergence of new alliances or partnerships related to research and development. These new alliances include university-industry contracts, such as between Monsanto and Washington University in St. Louis; industry-based consortia such as the Microelectronics & Computer Technology Corporation; and state government-university -industry programs such as Pennsylvania's Ben Franklin Partnership Program (Feller, 1987, p. 13).

Apart from the above general meaning of the knowledge complementarity, the knowledge complementarity in vertical integration can be explained in the following two ways. First, "vertical" means the interindustry dependency between upstream and downstream industries in R & D. Second, "integration" refers to the efficiency of the firm's own R & D activity inside the firm. The following two sections explain these two aspects.

3.1.2   The Modes of Knowledge Complementarity

Following Williamson's statement that the "informational economies of a firm are attributable to the way of information flows per se and veracity effects" (1971, p. 114), we will explain the knowledge complementarity effect through the informational interdependency between vertically related production processes in this section, and through the veracity effects of the employment relationship in the next section.

The interindustry dependency between upstream and downstream industries in R & D is discussed by Nelson (1986). In his explanation of technical societies, he says that "technical societies also provide a way for industrial scientists from upstream and downstream industries to meet and exchange information." His remark indicates the importance of knowledge complementarity in R & D. The reason why the knowledge complementarity effect is expected more in vertically related industries than in horizontally related (the same) industry and non-related industries will now be discussed.

Knowledge complementarity is performed in the process of communication between persons who require one another's knowledge in order to produce a new knowledge. First of all, the nature of knowledge transfer is different than that of goods transfer. While a flow of goods from one person to another reduces the stocks of the former and increases the stocks of the latter, a flow of knowledge may increase the recipient's stock of knowledge without reducing the stock of the transmitter. This implies that every flow of knowledge may bring about an increase in the combined stock of knowledge (Machlup, 1980, p. 170). Since the knowledge in upstream and downstream industries are complementary to one another, free communication or knowledge transfer between them increases the stock of knowledge for both sides. In horizontally related industries, knowledge may overlap rather than complement since it is from the same industry. Therefore, their free communication will not lead to the same stock of knowledge as that found in the vertically related industries. In this regard, if it happens in the non-related industries, their stock of knowledge may increase as a result of free communication between them. But they will finally find that sharing knowledge is not of much use to them, if they were seeking complementary technology. In other words, in vertically integrated industries free communication not only increases the stock of knowledge but sharing their knowledge is very useful in the production of new knowledge. The same effect is expected in vertically integrated firms, as well.

A firm that produces more inputs and possesses more sales functions internally has a comparative advantage in developing a new output model and innovating a new technology.[2]   The interdependencies between the production stages will require mutual assistance in order to solve technological problems and develop new models. Armour and Teece (1980) ascribed the comparative advantage to "free communication and free transfer of persons in vertical integration" (p. 470). They pointed out that "vertical integration can enhance innovation through the sharing of technological information common to separate stages of an industry, through facilitating the implementation of new technology when complex interdependencies are involved and through the formulation of more astute research objectives" (1980, p. 470). We use the phrase "complementary information" rather than "common information" to emphasize that there is different but related information content between stages.   The employment of R & D personnel and expansion of production stages can generate knowledge spill-over to other employees through intra-firm transfer and free communication and to future innovation through inside accumulation of technology and the training of other persons.

Top managers in the computer industry realize this knowledge complementarity effect in their in-house production of semi-conductors. For instance, Eric Bloch of National Science Foundation (NSF) and formerly of IBM has pointed out that "superior designs are usually obtained when the communications between system and component designers are open, when problems are rapidly identified, and where proper design trade-offs can be realized. Frequently, the synergetic effect is improved when both reside in the same organization."[3]   David Crockett of Hewlett-Packard's General Systems Division has stated that "we have tried to place IC facilities very close to the user group to match the technology with the problem to be solved."[4]   They represent the view that the vertical integration of input and output production will set up the stage for knowledge complementarity between R & D and production functions.

Besides in-house production of input and output, possessing more sales functions inside the firm bears another knowledge complementarity effect. Kline and Rosenberg state that "successful innovation requires a design that balances the requirements of the new product and its manufacturing processes, the marketing needs, and the need to maintain an organization that can continue to support all these activities effectively" (1986, p. 277). According to Kline and Rosenberg, attention to and prompt action on "feedback signals" from users are an important, often critical, part of innovation. In the traditional model one does research, research then leads to development, development to production, and production to marketing in the linear order. In their recently published "Chain-Linked Model" (1986), feedback links the whole step from research to marketing in innovation. Applying their model to our argument allows us to draw the following figure in order to explain the entire knowledge complementarity effect occurring in the vertically integrated firm's innovation.

There are five different mechanisms by which "free communication and free transfer of persons" within a firm leads to the knowledge complementarity effect of vertical integration. In Figure 1, a firm has two vertically related production processes -- upstream and downstream -- and a marketing function. Each process has the two divisions of R & D and production. Mechanism (a) represents the joint R & D of upstream and downstream production processes. The joint R & D produces economies of scale or scope in R & D through free communication and free transfer of persons. Mechanism (b) produces know-how complementarity of the two processes in production activity. Mechanism (c) produces an informational complementarity between the research division and the production division of different processes on both research and production activity. Mechanism (d) and (e) refer to the

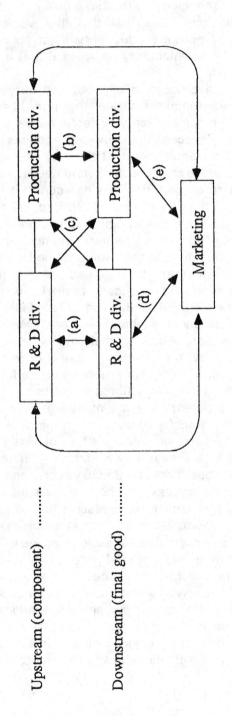

Figure 1: :   The Modes of Knowledge Complementarity

feedback effect from marketing to R & D and production. These five effects basically constitute what we call the knowledge complementarity effect. These effects do not work separately but cooperate together for the firm's best interests.[5]

In this study, we confine our knowledge complementarity effect to the ones affecting innovative activity. In other words, the economies of scope in R & D from mechanism (a), the complementarity effect on R & D from mechanism (c), and the feedback effect of marketing from mechanism (d) are included in the concept of the knowledge complementarity effect. The entire mechanism's cooperative effect on R & D is also included in that concept.

The modes of knowledge complementarity effect has been explained thus far in the context of the interindustry dependency between upstream and downstream production processes. In the next section the underlying reason for why the integrated state of a firm is good for R & D will be explained with the veracity effect of employment relationship.

3.1.3 Free Communication and the Employment Relationship

In this section we will show that the employment relationship is better than the contract relationship for the performance of R & D. The reason will be explained in the contexts of the informational advantage of a firm, the importance of communication in R & D, and the characteristics of the employment relationship.

About the informational advantages of a firm, Williamson (1975) says, "internal auditors are believed to have superior access to the information necessary for decision-making," and Arrow (1975) sees integration as "essentially a way of acquiring predictive information." Their view is well presented in Crocker's (1983) statement that "an integrated firm has more information at its disposal upon which payoffs may be conditioned" (p. 236), and

Masten's (1986) note that "among the advantages believed to arise under integration are better access to information and greater managerial control and flexibility" (p. 5). The firm's informational advantages lead to the argument that vertical integration provides a better environment for future innovation through the knowledge complementarity effect.

The knowledge complementarity effect is obtained through free communication and free transfer of persons within a firm.[6]   Communication means transfer of knowledge. Since transfer of knowledge is to a large extent "a person-to-person process" (Machlup, 1980), different forms of the person-to-person relationship need to be examined to explain the knowledge complementarity effect of vertical relationship. The externality effect of knowledge complementarity and the transaction costs related to it are the opposite sides of the same coin. If there is more room for opportunistic behavior, integration may produce bigger externality effect through veracity effect of employment relationship. Therefore, after we review the theory of the firm, we will introduce Masten's explanation of the characteristics of employment relationship relative to contract relationship.

There have been broadly three different approaches to viewing a firm: technical approach, contractual approach, and institutional approach. Arrow-Hahn (1971) and Debreu (1959) represent the technical approach by viewing a firm as a producer who chooses and carries out a production plan with inputs and outputs. In their field of general equilibrium analysis a firm is only one of the agents in the price system. The approach, however, provides little insight on the internal working of a firm or contractual modes. Alchian and Demsetz (1972) stress the internal relationship in a firm between entrepreneur (firm) and employee in their contractual approach. They emphasize team production, where each worker's productivity is not distinguishable and thus assume that workers have the incentive to "shirk." Therefore, a firm is an organizational structure where the entrepreneur (firm) monitors the input suppliers' (employees') shirking. In the institutional approach, Coase (1937) and Williamson (1975) define a firm as an internal market which transaction costs differentiate from external market. In their view the internal organization of a firm -- which can attenuate the transaction costs -- is basically an "employer-employee" relationship. This institutional approach leads to our argument that the employment relationship is better (more efficient) than the contract relationship in R & D. In other words, the employment relationship is expected to produce the externality effect in R & D activity through open-minded free communication either between employer and employee or among employees themselves. The reason can be explained in the same way that Masten (1986) explains the way the employment relationship can attenuate transaction costs. He examines the status of the employment relationship in the legal system and compares it to the commercial contract as follows:

1) The essential feature of the employment relationship is that the employer has the authority to direct some dimension of the employee's behavior (Coase, 1937; Simon, 1961). Although the employer can direct the way in which output is produced, an independent contractor may use any means whereby his work is to be done. Related to this, every employee accepts an implied duty to yield obedience to all reasonable rules, orders, and instructions from the employer.

2) There is generally a legal requirement that the employee act in the employer's interest. Therefore, termination is not the only sanction available to the employer: the employee can be held liable for damages to the employer's interests.

3) Managerial directives in a firm possess a presumptive validity that is reflected in the rules governing conflicts between employers and employees (Williamson, 1985). To the contrary, the contractual relationship requires a mutual consent in resolving disputes. Therefore, the employment relationship promotes responsive adaptation to changing circumstances.

4) Whereas one party to a business transaction is not liable to the other for harm caused by his failure to disclose facts of which he knows the other is ignorant, in

the employment relationship the employee is legally obligated to reveal relevant information to the employer.

5) The employer bears liability for harm caused by employees to the third party.

6) Employers have wide latitude in the suspension of employment contracts: the contract may be discharged on the basis of employee indolence, dishonesty, disloyalty, or disrespect.

7) In the commercial contract the burden of proof rests on the buyer to demonstrate that the contract was not met. But in the employment contract the burden rests on the employee to show that his behaviour was in fact satisfactory.

All the above characteristics indicate that the employment relationship is distinctively different from the contract relationship. The fourth characteristic, in particular, shows that the communication of relevant information is required in the employment relationship and thus the firm as a whole gets the superior access to information. Considering all these aspects, we can conclude that, in light of R & D characteristics such as uncertainty and human capital intensiveness, a larger knowledge complementarity effect is expected from the employment relationship than from the contractual relationship.

Another advantage of vertical integration in R & D activity is that, as Teece (1987) mentions, the production facility itself is an essential complementary asset for commercial innovation. After the early stage of innovation when prices become increasing important, mass production for economies of scale and timely supply of inputs become critical. This means that in-house production of input is an important complementary asset in the commercial success of innovation. Therefore, although this fact is not directly related to our main concern of examining "inside the black box" of innovative activity, it is indirectly related to R & D activity due to the fact that realizing the positive effect of vertical integration on commercial success of innovation will ensure the firm's increased next period R & D investment since the profitability of the investment has been raised.

This section described how vertical integration

provides a technologically supportive environment for innovative activity. It has provided a theoretical background for the technological relationship $FI_{t+1} = f(VI_t)$, where FI_{t+1} denotes future innovation, which means future outcome of innovative activity, and VI_t denotes the degree of vertical integration in the present. In the next section we will explain the economic reason for the choice of vertical integration over external sources in the firm's expected future innovation.

3.2 TRANSACTION COSTS OF TECHNOLOGY TRANSACTION

3.2.1 Asymmetric Information in Technology Transaction

In this section, we argue that any endeavor to obtain the technology itself or knowledge complementarity through relevant contracts in the market (which means technology licensing or R & D contracting), will likely result in large transaction costs relative to purchasing a tangible product or physical complementarity. We will explain that the transaction costs are the economic reason for the selection of vertical integration in expected future innovation.

According to the transaction cost literature, there are four basic conditions which together generate market transaction costs: asset specificity, uncertainty, opportunism, and bounded rationality. A technology market generally satisfies these four basic conditions.

First, a technology market satisfies the environmental conditions of asset specificity and uncertainty. Asset specificity is inferred from the fact that certain types of technology market may have small numbers of buyers and sellers. According to Williamson (1975), since technological information is often acquired only by the operation of a particular production process, this learning-by-doing puts only a small number of individuals in the position of being able to supply information about the technology. For buyers, the users of a specific technology are frequently confined to a small number, and only a few firms have the absorptive capabilities for the technology. Uncertainty is abundant in this market, because the nature of technology as a transferable product has the problem of information asymmetry between buyer and seller. Information asymmetry is a specific characteristic in technology transaction; this will be dealt with in detail later.

Second, since technology transaction in the market is basically technology transfer between individual agents, the human factors such as opportunism and bounded rationality are more involved in the technology market than in any other markets. Machlup (1980) stressed opportunism involved in the technology market by saying that "The difficulties (of knowledge transfer) become almost insuperable if the owners of the know-how are determined to keep it secret" (Vol. 3, p. 183).

Information asymmetry between buyer and seller is a fundamental problem in technology transactions. Because the information about the technology is the product itself, technology sellers will not want to disclose full information about their products to potential buyers until all the necessary transactions are completed to protect the proprietary value of the product. Arrow pointed this out when he said that "its value for the purchaser is not known until he has the information, but then he has in effect acquired it without cost" (1962, p. 615). He calls this the "fundamental paradox" of information. That is, technology is transacted under the circumstance in which the seller knows all of the contents of the technology while buyer does not know much.[7] This information asymmetry problem may be called simply a "quantification problem," because buyers do not know, for example, how accurate the consulting firm's information is and how much information is actually being provided.[8] In a technologically sophisticated inputs transaction, there also is an information asymmetry between the buyer and seller, because the buyer does not know the exact quality of intermediate goods at the time of transaction. These informational asymmetries in transaction lead either to market failure (Akerlof, 1970) or to a Pareto inefficient contract due to opportunistic behavior on the part of the private information holder (Crocker, 1983).

Crocker (1983) provides a theoretical background with regard to the asymmetric information argument of vertical integration. His model clearly shows that a downstream firm's private information about its productivity results in Pareto inefficient contracts on intermediate good transactions. Likewise, an upstream firm's private information about the quality of its product also results in a Pareto inefficient contract which creates the endogenous transaction costs ΔT_2 in Table 1.

There are two kinds of transaction costs involved in technology-related transactions. One, ΔT_1 in Table 1, is the exogenous transaction cost which occurs during the transaction process. The exogenous transaction cost refers to the contractual difficulty of buying technology or getting knowledge service from the seller's human capital. The other, which is ΔT_2 in Table 1, is the endogenous transaction cost which refers to the economic inefficiency in non-Pareto optimal production of the component (technology) and the final good after the agreement in the transaction contract.

Because centralized decision-making can solve the problem of the purchaser's inability to judge the value and optimal use of the technology or its related products in advance, vertical integration can be expected to reduce these transactional dilemmas by relieving the condition of information asymmetry, by adjusting payoffs to the previously distinct firms, and by attenuating the incentives for opportunistic behavior.[9]

Teece (1980) explained a firm's diversification in terms of the transaction cost argument. In his example of the diversification of oil companies, he argued that the asymmetric information problem in a technology transaction made oil companies extend their activity to other energy sources such as uranium or coal rather than sell their technology in the market. While his argument focused on selling the technology, we examine the transaction cost involved in buying technology or getting technology service for innovative activity.

Mowery (1983) explains the asymmetric information problem of technology-related transactions in the model of R & D contracting. He says that contractual difficulties due to imperfect knowledge, opportunistic behavior due to specialized research service, and the need for means of absorbing and modifying technologies from external sources lead to in-house research activity as a complement to external research activity.

Anderson and Schmittlein (1984) empirically test the hypothesis that the difficulty in evaluating a sales person's performance leads to vertical integration in the form of a direct sales force. They got good empirical results to support the view that the transaction costs related to the difficulty of evaluating performance lead to vertical integration. Crockett of Hewlett-Packard supports this view:

> An in-house capability of semi-conductor
> also helps in keeping our suppliers a bit
> more honest .... We believe having our own
> facility helps us control the quality of the
> end product, even though we buy about
> 90% outside.[10]

While information asymmetry is the most important source of the transaction costs, we will explain that the problem of opportunistic behavior is another important source of the transaction costs related to the external R & D activity.

3.2.2 Human Capital and Opportunism

Even if recognition of the value of the technology is no problem and buyers concede value, there is still another problem in technology transactions. Technology seldom comes only in the form of a chemical compound or the blue print for a special device. It is not just information that can be expressed and understood easily through a sheet of blue print. In most technology transfers, skilled and specialized manpower is needed for interpretation and embodiment. That is, human capital from the seller is needed to help and facilitate the execution of the actual transfer itself. This means that the buyer is exposed to the risk that the seller might render promised transfer assistance in a perfunctory fashion. This fact is well presented in Machlup's following remark:

> If the patented invention cannot be used without complementary know-how, the owners may be in the fortunate position of enjoying both patent protection and the protection of his secret technological knowledge .... Little can be done to achieve the transfer if the owner of the know-how is not willing to give up his secrets. (1980, Vol. 3, pp. 183-184)

He indicates the difficulty of technology transfer and implies the strong potential for opportunistic behavior by the seller in the market.

Teece (1987) has also mentioned the same problem of opportunistic behavior in his study of complementary assets in commercial innovation:

> In strategic (contractual) partnering, there is the risk that the partner will not perform according to the innovator's perception of what the contract requires; there is the added danger that the partner may imitate the innovator's technology and attempt to compete with the innovator. (p. 79)

All of these problems stem from the same source such that the object of the transaction is "information, knowledge, or know-how" which is embodied in the human capital. It seems to be true that there is more room for opportunistic behavior as more human capital is involved in the market transaction. According to Williamson (1975, 1985), there are two types of opportunistic behavior; one is selective or distorted information disclosure and the other is false or empty promises regarding future conduct. Since integration eliminates transaction costs due to opportunistic behavior, we hypothesize that integration is a better institutional mode than contracting for R & D activity, which is human capital-intensive. As an answer to the criticisms how we can expect to have selfless humans rather than selfish ones just by mere integration, the advantages of employment relationship will be utilized. As explained in the previous chapter, since the employment relationship is more tied-up and has more strict rights and responsibilities, there are administrative solutions to employees' opportunistic behavior. Also, there are likely to be fewer selfish employees in the integrated firm, because we assume that the agents who pursued their separate profit maximization before the integration are now seeking their joint profit maximization after integration.

3.2.3 Integration and Technology Leakages

Vertical integration also may be an effective method to keep a new technology from leaking to other competitors. According to Mansfield (1985), the information about the nature and operation of the new product or process is in the hands of at least some of their rivals within about a year, on the average, after a new product is developed (p. 220). One of the most important channels through which this information spreads is input suppliers and output users or distributors, since they can be in a position to pass on relevant technical information to competitive firms (Mansfield, 1985, p. 221).

Furthermore, if the new product is highly sophistigated, the seller may need to provide some information about the product to the buyers which may permit information leakages through "reverse engineering." As more communication and interaction with other firms is required in the development of a new product or process, the more likely it is that the information required to develop an equivalent technology leaks and the competitors will rapidly enter the market with an imitative product.

Vertical integration may mitigate this problem of technology leakages by preventing input suppliers and/or customers from obtaining and spreading the relevant information to others. The common ownership of integrated production processes, by reducing the amount of information sellers need to reveal in order to obtain sales, may be a desirable strategy to limit information leakages to competitors.

A related argument has been presented by Teece (1986), who maintains that integrating rather than contracting for upstream and downstream activities is likely to be the optimal strategy for gaining complementary assets if the technology is easily imitated (p. 293). In strategic partnerships for complementary assets, the contractor may use the relationship to gain access to the technology and imitate the innovator's technology earlier than other competitors. This, of course, is just a particular form of opportunism, a general problem which we have already addressed. Vertical integration, therefore, may be a strategy to keep a new technology completely "in house" and to mitigate the leakage of proprietary information.

In this section we explained the sources of the transaction costs related to technology licensing or externally contracted R & D. The transaction costs are the economic reason for firms' selection of vertical integration over external sources in expectation of future innovation. That is, this section has provided a theoretical background for the behavioral relationship, $VI_t = g(E_t(FI_{t+1}))$, where VI_t is today's level of vertical integration and $E_t(FI_{t+1})$ is the expected level of future innovation.

3.3 SUMMARY

In this chapter we explained two basic important notions: the knowledge complementarity effect of vertical integration and the transaction costs of a technology transaction.

The difference between the knowledge complementarity effect associated with vertical integration and that associated with horizontal integration or conglomerates was examined. Free communication and free transfer of persons were explained to be the tools for various modes of knowledge complementarity. The informational advantage of a firm and the characteristics of the employment relationship were examined in detail to provide the basis for free communication within a firm.

The transaction costs which will inevitably occur during the external acquisition of the knowledge complementarity effect were explained in two different terms: the asymmetric information problem of technology transaction and the opportunistic behavior of human capital. These two conditions generate transaction costs for a firm when R & D contracting or external acquisition of technology is used for the purpose of obtaining the knowledge complementarity effect in external market. The knowledge complementarity effect and the relevant transaction costs are the opposite sides of the same coin. Integration produces the knowledge complementarity effect which is an externality effect. But using an external market for this effect will incur transaction costs.

The question of why all firms do not vertically integrate for their efficient R & D must also be considered. The main reasons are the internalization costs,[11] and especially bureaucratic costs are huge because more human capital is involved in the internally R & D-intensive firm. The high internalization cost of human capital is well presented in Masten's (1982) remark that "since human capital cannot be internalized in the same way that physical capital can, rent-seeking cannot be entirely expunged and conflicts therefore continue to require arbitration" (p. 43).

In summary, we propose two empirical hypotheses in this chapter.

Hypothesis 1: the more vertically integrated a firm is, the more efficient the firm's R & D activity is (through the knowledge complementarity effect). This hypothesis is represented in the function $FI_{t+1} = f(VI_t)$.

Hypothesis 2: the more a firm expects future innovation to be significant, the more the firm vertically integrates today (because using external market incurs huge transaction costs). This hypothesis is represented in the function $VI_t = g(E_t(FI_{t+1}))$.

Notes

1. When we checked a recently published book (Ravenscraft and Scherer, 1987) about merger activity, we could not find any R & D-related rationales for merger in the book. Although there has been no recent data on R & D-related mergers, there are many recent merger cases which are apparently technology related. In particular, most of acquisitions in the semi-conductor industry and software industry are technology related. For example, Schlumberger Ltd. bought Fairchild Camera & Instrument Corp. to gain a technological base to expand into the semi-conductor industry (Business Week, December 3, 1979, p. 69), and Management Sciences America (MSA) bought a manufacturing software producer Arista from Xerox to obtain "people's talents" (Datamation, July 1, 1986, p. 68).

2. There may be a threshold in the effect of vertical integration on innovation, as Scherer (1980) found it in the firm size's effect on innovation. We will test this hypothesis empirically by using a semi-log function later.

3. Obilichetti, 1982, p. 6-3

4. Datamation, June 1979, p. 103

5. While the knowledge complementarity effect of owning successive production stages is our rationale for vertical integration as an environment for future innovation, Carlton (1979) presents another reason that a vertically integrated firm is more likely to adopt a new socially beneficial technology than a nonintegrated firm. He says that without vertical integration, price signals are not sufficient to make the firm adopt the new technology. His argument is simply that control and coordination between successive production stages make the integrated firm introduce the new production technology easily. Although Carlton's argument supports our view of vertical integration as an

environment for future innovation, our study goes beyond his perspective to argue that a new technology can be created as well as introduced more efficiently in a vertically integrated firm than in a nonintegrated firm.

6. Again, as it is in footnote 4 in chapter 1, we exclude the notion of negative knowledge in this study. Therefore, we assume that firms circulate only "relevant" and "efficient" information.

7. According to Hippel (1987), informal know-how trading has a lower transaction cost than more formal agreements to license or sell similar information, because it is traded by knowledgeable engineers (p. 300).

8. An organizational remedy for the quantification problem is incentive-based contracts with external suppliers of knowledge. Consulting is akin to the purchase of consumer durables. The supplier's interest in repeat business and reputation is the effective spur to quality.

9. For the criticisms centering on how integration transforms selfish humans into selfless ones, most economists cite the existence of administrative solutions as an answer (Masten, 1986). Besides that, we cannot disregard a firm's nature such as joint profit maximization of all the agents within a firm. On the other hand, the problem of subgoal pursuit by employees within a firm remains a task for economists (Williamson, 1975; Leibenstein, 1979; Radner, 1985).

10. Datamation, June 1979, p. 103

11. The other reasons are that in-house production of inputs has the risk of technological obsolescence and it may not let the firm utilize the newly developed outside idea or parts.

IV
Vertical Integration and Technological Innovation in the U.S. Electronics Industry

4.1 INTRODUCTION

This chapter empirically examines the relationship between a firm's decision to integrate vertically and its R & D strategy. The first hypothesis to be estimated is that a vertically integrated firm is more efficient in R & D than other firms. The second hypothesis to be estimated is that the more future innovation a firm expects to have, the more the firm vertically integrates today. In estimating these hypotheses, we encounter a simultaneity effect which has been neglected by many economists. While expected future innovation is a determinant of vertical integration (through transaction costs), future innovation is itself a function of the degree of vertical integration (through knowledge complementarity effect). Therefore, future innovation and vertical integration are simultaneously determined. In this regard, the term "expected future innovation" means the expected improvement of R & D performance due to the rising degree of vertical integration.

As the previous literature (Armour and Teece, 1980) has stated, the second hypothesis can be investigated by testing the first hypothesis through a model in which innovative output is a function of vertical integration. But the argument that vertical integration has an impact on innovative performance is not the same as the argument that expected innovative performance is a determinant of vertical integration. They are two different stories: the first is about what factors determine innovative performance and

42

the second is about what factors affect the decision to integrate vertically.   In other words, while the first hypothesis is about the technological relationship between environmental factors and innovative output inside the "black box" of knowledge production (innovative output), the second hypothesis is about the behavioral relationship that a firm vertically integrates because of the high level of expected future innovation. Based on this fact, we will use a two-equation system to explain our main hypothesis about the determinants of vertical integration.

Our model is composed of two equations:

$$VI_t = f(E_t(FI_{t+i})) \text{ and } FI_{t+i} = g(VI_t),$$

where i is a nonnegative integer.

The FI equation represents the first hypothesis that the productivity of a given R & D dollar will be higher for the more vertically integrated firms than for the less vertically integrated firms because vertical integration provides the effect of knowledge complementarity in innovative activity. The VI equation represents our main hypothesis that expected future innovation is a determinant of vertical integration because of transaction cost considerations.

The FI equation should be estimated before the VI equation, because the FI equation provides the technological relationship for a firm to form an expectation on future innovation. If the first hypothesis does not hold, we can not theorize the simultaneity of vertical integration and R & D strategy, and can not test empirically the second equation which has an expectation variable. Therefore, in this chapter we will examine empirically the FI equation first, and if it holds then we will proceed to estimate the VI equation.

In estimating the VI equation we encounter the problems of simultaneity effect between VI and E(FI), and the unobservableness of expectation variable E(FI). To solve these problems we use the dynamic simultaneous equation model that includes both the VI and FI equations. In the remaining part of this section we will investigate the stability condition of this model and the OLS estimate's bias.

Linearize both equations to obtain:

$$VI_t = a_0 + a_1 E_t(FI_{t+1}) + u_t$$

$$FI_{t+1} = b_0 + b_1 VI_t + \eta_{t+1}$$

Since $E_t(FI_{t+1})$ has a positive effect on VI_t and VI_t also has a positive effect on FI_{t+1} for our hypotheses, the parameters a_1 and b_1 should be positive.

Most economic theorizing has necessarily been about equilibrium positions (Johnston, 1984, p. 4); the existence of stability (of the equilibrium) is, in fact, assumed in the process of estimation in the time series model (Kmenta, 1971, p. 593). As we can see in Figure 2, we need to impose the restriction

$$1 / a_1 > b_1$$

so that the equilibrium of our model is stable over time. After estimating the model, we will test if this stability condition holds. In Figure 2, if the disturbances were both zero ($u_t = 0 = \eta_{t+1}$), the model would be represented by F and V lines. Nonzero disturbances would shift the curves up or down from the equilibrium position to generate a scatter of observations around the VI_t^*, FI_{t+1}^* point.

The FI equation plays two different roles in estimating the VI equation. First, it enables $E_t(FI_{t+1})$ to be transformed into a function of all observable variables so that the VI equation can be estimated. The process will be shown later in section 5 of this chapter. Second, even if $E_t(FI_{t+1})$ is observable, there is another problem of simultaneity effect in the VI equation. When we take an expectation on FI equation at time t, we get $E_t(FI_{t+1}) = b_0 + b_1 VI_t$. From the process that u_t affects VI_t in VI equation, and VI_t affects $E_t(FI_{t+1})$ in the above equations, we can see that $E_t(FI_{t+1})$ and u_t are correlated (simultaneity

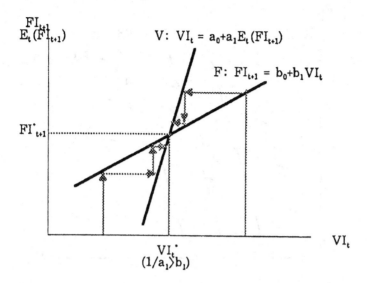

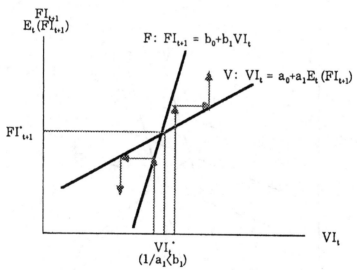

Figure 2: The Stable and Unstable Conditions
Sorce: Adapted from Johnston (1984, p. 444)

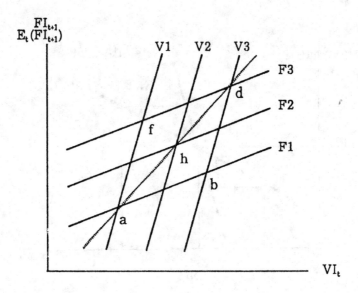

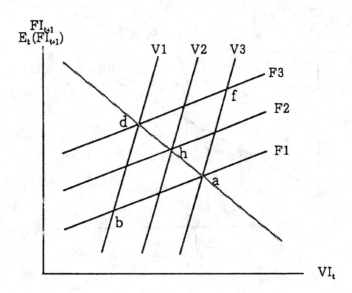

Figure 3: The Bias and Inconsistency of OLS Estimates
Sorce: Adapted from Judge et al. (1982, p. 347)

effect). If we estimate the VI equation using OLS, the estimator a_1 becomes biased and inconsistent as shown in Figure 3.

Nonzero disturbances and different values of a_0 and b_0 shift the F, V curves up or down. The observation data that would result from the equilibrium values of the system would be contained within the parallelogram a, b, f, d. The relation that will result (estimates of a_1) when OLS line passes through the equilibrium points a, h, and d, for example, will overstate or understate the magnitude of a_1(see, Judge et al., 1982, p. 347). Therefore, the estimation method of the simultaneous equation model should be used. When there is no time lag between FI and VI, $E_t(FI_t)$ becomes an observable variable. In this case we use the two-stage least squares (2SLS) estimation method to estimate VI equation. When there is a time lag between FI and VI, the two equation model is a recursive model with an unobservable expectation variable. In this case we use a nonlinear estimation method to estimate the VI equation. The correlation problem between an explanatory variable and disturbance term is automatically solved during the process of transforming the expectation variable into a function of observable variables.

4.2 THE SAMPLE

Broadly, there are two types of studies in the empirical literature on the subject of vertical integration. One type tests the applicability of the transaction cost approach to explaining the degree of vertical integration of a single firm or industry (Armour and Teece, 1980; Monteverde and Teece, 1982; Anderson and Schmittlein, 1984; Masten, 1984). The generalizability of these case study results is hard to establish, because the results are from a single firm or industry. The other type of study examines a broad base of industries to determine the relationship between vertical integration and such variables as industry concentration, firm size, sales growth, capital intensity, and R & D intensity (Adelman, 1955; Gort, 1962; Tucker and Wilder, 1977; Levy, 1985; MacDonald, 1985). But these studies do not apply to theories of vertical integration because they either use industry-level data (while integration is a firm-level decision) or they use insufficient proxies for the variables in their argument.

There have been various arguments about what level data should be used. While Tucker and Wilder (1977) examined the determinants of vertical integration across both industries and firms, their industry-level analysis was criticized by E. W. Eckard (1979). Eckard argued that because they used Census data, which is the aggregation of plant-level data, their industry-level study was confined to vertical integration within plants, and thus their measure systematically ignored other forms of firm-level vertical integration (e.g., mergers and new plant construction). Another argument stems from business economists such as Pennings, Hambrick, and MacMillan (1984) who want to subdivide the unit of study into the firm's divisions. Pennings, Hambrick, and MacMillan (1984) state that

> many companies operate in diverse markets, so perhaps the unit of study should be the firm or its divisions, depending on whether the firm is predominantly a single product organization or operates in various discrete markets. For example, the office products division of IBM might expand its service operations regardless of service policy of other divisions which operate in different and nonoverlaping markets. (p. 310)

They used PIMS (Profit Impact of Market Strategies) data base where the unit was a strategic business unit ("SBU"). SBU, which operates plants for its own sake, sells a distinct set of products to an identifiable set of customers in a clearly defined market. The disadvantage of PIMS data is that firm-level integration of mergers and new plant construction cannot be explained. For instance, a new semi-conductor plant which will supply both to the typewriter division and to the computer division of IBM, is wholly ignored by PIMS data.

Since we analyze vertical integration in a transaction cost framework, we confine our study to a firm-level analysis.[1] In transaction cost economics a firm is the relevant unit of analysis to be differentiated from market mechanisms. While a few economists have tried to explain the economics of the relationship between the firm's divisions (Leibenstein, 1979; Radner, 1985), the divisional relationship within a firm will be explained in the context of internalization cost in this paper. If the firm is organized according to divisions which maximize each division's profit, it will be hard to exclude the possibility of opportunistic behavior between them. But if the firm's highest managers can control and coordinate the divisions to maximize the firm-level profit, there will be little to worry about in the divisional relationship. In our analysis the risk of a division-specific decision being treated as a firm-level strategy can be minimized by our measure of vertical integration. This is because the measure of vertical integration, which is the ratio of value added to sales revenue, has relatively lower value as it becomes forward integration as compared to backward integration (see, e.g., Adelman [1955], pp. 282-283) and because forward integration tends to be a division-specific decision in the electronics industry, as in the previous example of service operations. In summary, when we use a firm as a unit of analysis, we have the advantage of explaining a firm-level integration. We also have the disadvantages that (1) a division-level integration may be counted as a firm-level integration, and (2) there may be transaction costs involved in the division-level transactions.

The empirical analysis in our study is conducted with firm-level data obtained primarily from the Annual Industrial File of Standard and Poor's Compustat tapes. This data was previously used in firm-level studies by Tucker and Wilder (1977) and by Levy (1981, 1985). While their sample included all manufacturing industries, we focus on the electronics industry which corresponds to the industry code number 3600's in Standard and Poor's Compustat tapes. There are some reasons for using the sample from a given industry rather than the whole industry. First, the inclusion of more industries in the data set will make the measure of innovative performance noisier, because each industry may have different propensity to patent its innovative output and different propensity to increase its R & D expenditure as the productivity of R & D increases. Kline and Rosenberg (1986) indicated that there are many black boxes rather than just one, because (1) the manner in which innovations are generated, (2) the state of knowledge in the relevant science and technology, and (3) the nature and the potential profitability of the output of the black box, differ significantly from industry to industry. Thus pouring equal incremental inputs into the black boxes of different industries is expected to yield very different rates of return on the resources invested. Therefore, we selected one industry which seems to be relevant to our study's purpose because it is very susceptible to technology change and tends to emphasize the acquisition and development of new technology.[2] Second, since our measure of vertical integration tends to be higher in backward integration, we can get a rather non-biased measure of vertical integration by studying the electronics industry whose firms are mainly engaged in the similar production stage of manufacturing final output than by studying the industry whose firms are engaged in the diverse stages from exploring to retailing. Our sample firms are not mainly involved in exploring, mining, producing basic material, distributing, wholesaling, or retailing.

Our data is unquestionably noisy, since it is composed of 15 diversified firms and their sample years are not the same. Because we have limited our study to sample firms that have high R & D to sales ratio, we are reluctant to study other industries such as the steel or petroleum industry. Even if those industries provided data homogeneity and all the relevant data items without missing value problem, the average ratio of R & D expenditure to sales for the firms in these industries is below 1% during the 1970s and 80s. It is less likely that the steel or petroleum industry may consider the aspect of technological innovation when they integrate vertically.

Eighty-seven companies were listed in the industry code number 3600's in Standard and Poor's Compustat tapes. Firms for which data were available to construct all the relevant variables for more than four consecutive years were included in the dataset. Although this method diminishes data homogeneity due to the year-specific effect of each firm's different time period, it can expand the number of sample firms to the maximum. We excluded the firms where the requisite data was missing for more than three consecutive years during the period, 1966-1986. In most cases, firms were excluded due to their failure to report expense items which are required to create the vertical integration measure. This editing process gave us 15 firms which include the no longer extant firms (Sprague Electric Co. and Cutler-Hammer Inc.), a young firm (Northern Telecom Ltd.) started in 1973, and the large firms that have survived the entire time span.

We will use pooled time-series, cross-sectional data. The sample spans 4 to 20 years and includes 15 firms. The company names, their main businesses, and the years of each company are shown in Table 3.

We used simple procedures to correct for missing values,[3] following Levy (1981). The sales variable was available for all the years and companies. For most of the expense items (used to construct value added), we calculated the percentage growth over the preceding two years and multiplied that by the value of the variable for the preceding year.[4] Since the ratio of labor to sales is expected to be relatively constant, a different procedure was used to correct for missing values of labor expense. The average labor/sales ratio was calculated for the preceding three years and then multiplied that by the current level of sales in order to get a value for the current labor expense. There was no problem of missing values for R & D expense during each firm's time span. The number of issued patents were available only until 1984. Using patent data as a variable limits the number of available observations.

Table 3: The List of Sample Companies

Gould Inc.	
(computers-mini & micro)	71-77
Bell & Howell Co.	
(computer peripherals)	67-81
Acme Electric Corp.	
(electric industrial apparatus)	72-86
Conchemco Inc.	
(industrial controls)	72-79
Cutler-Hammer Inc.	
(industrial controls)	71-77
Thomas Industries Inc.	
(electric lighting-wiring equip.)	74-78
Northern Telecom Ltd.	
(telephone & telegraph apparatus)	73-85
Raytheon Co. (search-navigating	
-guiding systems equip.)	67-86
Singer Co. (search-navigating	
-guiding systems equip.)	70-73
Texas Instruments Inc.	
(semi-conductor & related devices)	73-84
AMP Inc. (electronic components	
not elsewhere classified)	70-86
Thomas & Betts Corp. (electronic	
components not elsewhere classified)	67-77
Rogers Corp. (electronic components	
not elsewhere classified)	67-72
Sprague Electric Co. (electronic	
components not elsewhere classified)	66-73
Crouse-Hinds Co. (electric transmiss.	
& distribut. equip.)	70-75

4.3 THE VARIABLES

In forming the VI equation we chose the variables so as to be able to explain the important rationales for a high-tech firm's vertical integration such as the initial transaction cost T of the component itself, internalization cost C, demand uncertainty UI, and the transaction cost ΔT of R & D activity.

The VI equation is

$$VI_t = f\ (E_t(FI_{t+i}),\ VI_{t-1},\ CAP_t,\ FS_t,\ CASH_t,\ VAR_t).$$

$E_t(FI_{t+i})$ is the expected productivity or performance of R & D activity, VI_{t-1} is a lagged value of VI_t, CAP is capital intensity, FS is firm size, CASH is the ratio of liquidity or cash flow to sales, and VAR is unanticipated variance in firm sales. E(FI) is the variable of the transaction cost ΔT, because as firms expect significant future innovation, they integrate vertically to mitigate the expected transaction costs related to the innovation. CAP is the variable of the initial transaction cost T, since capital intensity is assumed to represent asset specificity although capital may be generic as well as specific. FS and CASH are the variables of internalization cost C, because we assume that there is managerial diseconomies of scale to firm size and the cash-to-sales ratio may be a measure of managerial efficiency. And VAR is the variable of demand uncertainty. A lagged VI variable is included in the equation to allow for the partial adjustment of vertical integration. The partial adjustment means that the actual change is only a fraction of the desired change, i.e.,

$$VI_t - VI_{t-1} = \delta\ (VI_t^* - VI_{t-1})$$

where VI^* is the desired vertical integration and $0 < \delta < 1$. Also, VI^* is a function of expected future innovation $E_t(FI_{t+i})$ so that we have

$$VI_t^* = a + \beta\ E_t(FI_{t+i}).$$

Then by combining these two equations we get

$$VI_t - VI_{t-1} = \delta (\alpha + \beta E_t(FI_{t+i}) - VI_{t-1})$$

$$\text{or } VI_t = \alpha \delta + \beta \delta E_t(FI_{t+i}) + (1 - \delta)VI_{t-1}$$

Thus we estimate a regression equation of VI_t on $E_t(FI_{t+i})$ and VI_{t-1} (see Maddala [1977], pp. 142-143).

The FI equation is

$$FI_{t,1} = g (VI_t, FI_t, LCAP_t \text{ or } CAP_t, FS_t, LCASH_t \text{ or } CASH_t, R\&D_t),$$

where FI_t is a lagged value of FI_{t+1}, $LCASH_t$ is the level of cash flow, and $R\&D_t$ is the amount of R & D expenditure. This equation can be called the knowledge production function which translates past research expenditures (R & D) through firm-specific environmental factors (VI, FS, LCAP, LCASH) into inventions. A lagged FI variable is also a kind of firm-specific environmental factor, since it can be a useful proxy for the firm's technological endowment from the past R & D activity.

Vertical integration refers to the extent to which a firm carries within itself on the production processes from raw materials to final product (Singer, 1968). There are two different ways to measure vertical integration at the firm level. One is the number of distinct stages of production in a firm (Armour and Teece, 1980). The other is the ratio of the value added of these inputs produced within the firm relative to the value of the final product (Adelman, 1955; Tucker and Wilder, 1977; Levy, 1985).

Measuring vertical integration in terms of distinct stages is arbitrary from a theoretical viewpoint. First, classifying each distinct production stage in the whole production process is arbitrary in nature. Second, no matter how detailed the classification of the production stages is, there still remains the problem of different degrees of integration among the stages. Furthermore, detailed data regarding the production by firms in different stages is generally not available in publicly accessible data sources for most industries (Levy, 1981).

Thus in this study we measure vertical integration as the ratio of value added to sales. The rationale for this measure is that value added may be viewed as the difference between sales and purchased material inputs (i.e., inputs other than labor and capital). Hence, backward integration will tend to reduce the purchases of material inputs while leaving sales of final outputs constant, with a resulting increase in the ratio of value added to sales. Similarly in forward integration, sales will tend to increase while leaving the purchased material inputs constant, also resulting in an increase in the ratio of value added to sales (Tucker and Wilder, 1977, p. 83).

But there are some obvious disadvantages to using the value added/sales ratio as an index of vertical integration:

1) The index is not very useful for cross-sectional comparisons because the measure depends on the stage of production at which the output is being sold. The firm producing input will have the higher ratio of value added/sales than the firm producing the final output even though there is no difference in the actual amount of integration for the firms. Let us take an example from Adelman (1955) to see this.

> Suppose that in a given industry there are three firms: a primary production firm, a manufacturing firm, and a distribution firm; each contributes one-third of total value added by the industry. The primary producer -- on the unrealistic assumption that he buys nothing from other firms -- would have a ratio of 1.0; the manufacturer, a ratio of .50; the distributor, one of .33. (p. 282)

2) The index becomes higher as the firm integrates

backward to input production rather than forward to distribution stage. Thus the index is not very useful for intertemporal comparisons for a given firm because the integration can take place either upstream or downstream. Again Adelman explains this from the same example.

> If the manufacturer integrated backward to absorb primary production, the new firm would have a ratio of 1.0; if he integrated forward to absorb distribution, the new firm would have a ratio of .67. (p. 283)

3) Value added includes accounting profit, which varies among firms and times for many reasons other than differences in the degree of vertical integration.

4) The ratio is sensitive to changes in the price of input and output over time. Despite its limitations, the value added/sales measure of vertical integration is employed in our study, because it is the most commonly used measure in the studies of vertical integration and it is closer to the definition of vertical integration than the number of production stages within a firm.

In our empirical study we managed to reduce the limitations of the value added/sales measure. First, we picked a specific industry (electronics industry) in which most firms' main business is manufacturing. Second, we investigated a firm's behavior over time by introducing firm dummies to have the less biased measure of the value added/sales ratio, because in intertemporal comparisons each firm's initial production stage before integration is given. Third, in order to correct short-term changes in profitability we took the averages of vertical integration over a prescribed number of years.[5]

Since neither value added nor the cost of purchased materials is available as a separate data item on the Compustat tapes, we constructed our measure of value added by summing up the major items that comprise value added. These items are labor and related expense,[6] depreciation and amortization, fixed charges (interest expense), income taxes, net income after taxes, and rental expense. The same method was used in the previous literature (Tucker and Wilder, 1977; Levy, 1981).

Future innovation (FI) is defined as an outcome or performance of the present research activity which will occur at a later date. Since the basic assumption is that vertical integration may induce superior innovative performance, an appropriate measure of FI would be the value of innovations produced by the R & D program normalized by the level of R & D expenditures (Armour and Teece, 1980). Because the numerator of the ratio is impossible to obtain, we use three different proxies of FI in this study: the number of issued patents, the amount of R & D expenditures, and the ratio of R & D expenditure to sales.

Even if patents data are a direct indicator of the outcome of the research activity, they are an imperfect indicator of new inventions. This is because patents are not the only output from R & D activity -- they measure only a fraction of this output -- and also because the differences in patent quality are not considered. The patent system itself may be a relatively unimportant factor in the research and development strategy of some firms (Hall, Griliches and Hausman, 1984). Many patents may or may not be commercialized and sometimes individuals and firms do not patent for fear of information leakage (to keep the underlying technology secret).[7]

On the other hand, even if R & D expenditure is only an input to R & D activity, the expenditure data can be viewed as a useful proxy for the expected return on innovative activity. This is because as firms expect that the productivity per dollar of research expenditure in vertically integrated firms will be higher, such firms will devote more resources to R & D (Armour and Teece, 1980, p. 471).[8]

With regard to the value term, R & D expenditure data may be better than patents data in representing the degree of research performance or the productivity of research activity. While patents data count only the integer number of technical research outcomes regardless of the economic value, R & D expenditure data can represent the economic value of any research outcome in monetary terms even if the research outcome does not result in an issued patent. Suppose that a firm's research productivity has been improved a lot to produce a new research outcome by vertical integration. Although this new result of research activity is not sure to have a patent on it, as long as the result is economically valuable to the firm, this firm will devote more resources to R & D because it realizes that research investment is more productive than before.

R & D intensity is another useful proxy for innovative performance. This is R & D expenditure normalized by sales. Since firm-size effects can be excluded by this measure, even small firms may have greater R & D intensity than big firms, if their degree of vertical integration is greater than that of the big firms, and if they realize that their vertical integration helps the innovation.

When patents are used as a measure of FI, R & D expenditure becomes a financial input to research activity, and thus the most important explanatory variable for FI. When we use R & D expenditure as a measure of FI, we use only environmental resources of VI, FS, and LCASH as determinants of FI.

One question that arises concerns how many time lags should be imposed between the environmental factors and research output. When patents are used for FI, the process of R & D activity can be drawn as the following:

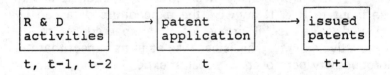

The R & D activity is proceeded under the influence of the environmental factors such as VI, FS, and LCASH. Since there has been no research to examine the time lag between environmental factors and research output, the research on the time lag between R & D expenditure and patent application will be consulted. That is, we assume that the change of R & D environment will have the same or smaller time lag than the change of R & D expenditure in affecting R & D output, because environmental factors have an effect on the path from financial input to the research outcome. Schmookler (1966) found that the strongest correlation occurred when patent applications were lagged two years after the year of investment. According to Hall, Griliches, and Hausman (1983,1984), a significant effect of R & D expenditure on patent application was found mainly in the first year. That is, empirically they found that no time lag existed between R & D expenditure and patent application. They stated that the reason for their failure to find a longer lag structure was due to the fact that successful research led both to a patent application and to a commitment of funds for applied research and development expenditure which held most of the R & D expenditure within large corporations. This implies that environmental factors will affect patent application with the time lag of either 0, 1, or 2 years. If the firm decides the next period's R & D investment at the time when it sees the R & D output (i.e., patent application), it is also implied that environmental factors have the same time lag of either 0, 1, or 2 to affect R & D expenditure when R & D expenditure is used for FI. Since it took 19 months on average for a patent application to mature into an issued patent during the mid-1970s (Scherer, 1982, p. 229),[9] the whole time lag between R & D environment and patent issuance will be 1, 2, or 3 years. Thus when we use issued patents for FI, we estimate the model with the time lag of either 1, 2, or 3 years between FI and VI. When we use R & D expenditure for FI, we estimate it with the time lag of 0, 1, or 2 years between them.

The variable VI as a determinant of FI implies that vertical integration leads to a better R & D performance through the knowledge complementarity effect. The variable E(FI) as a determinant of VI means that expected R & D activity is a factor to be considered at the time of VI decision because a lot of the transaction cost in the process of R & D activity is expected to be saved by VI. Therefore, the expected signs of VI in the FI equation and of E(FI) in the VI equation are positive.

Data of each firm's number of issued patents was obtained from the annual "Index of Patents" published by U.S. Patent and Trademark office. R & D expenditure data is obtained from the Standard and Poor's Compustat tapes.[10]

CAP is measured as the ratio of fixed assets to sales.[11] This represents asset specificity, because the higher the capital intensity is, the more the resources of the firm tend to be immobile. Asset specificity increases the initial transaction cost T of the component itself, because it reflects the greater potential for opportunistic behaviour in idiosyncratic transactions. MacDonald (1985) has stated:

> In the transactions cost approach, the potential costs of market failure due to small numbers bargaining conditions are magnified in capital intensive industries, since the firm's large initial investment is sunk. (p. 328)

Therefore, the expected sign of this variable in VI equation is positive.

CAP also is used in the FI equation when R & D intensity is used as a measure of FI. Since high capital intensity helps the firm's research activity through its relatively extensive manufacturing infrastructure, CAP is expected to have a positive sign in the FI equation, too. With the same reason, level of capital (LCAP) is assumed to be a positive factor in determining FI when patents or R & D expenditure is used for FI.

A firm's size (FS) is measured by the firm's sales for a given year. This variable represents the managerial costs of internal control. As a firm's size increases, managerial efficiency decreases, and thus the internalization cost C increases. That is, we assume that managerial diseconomies of scale to firm size. Even if there may be managerial economies of scale up to a certain firm size, we disregard this fact because any firms which file 10-K's are already big firms.

Williamson (1975, ch. 7) provides the following

rationales for limits of vertical integration related to firm size: (1) Bounded rationality gives rise to finite spans of control together with the specialization of communication and decision-making functions and thus radial expansion of the enterprise causes "control loss phenomenon;" (2) Increasing firm size leads to taller hierarchies in which leaders are less subject to control by lower-level participants or stock holders and thus results in the inefficiency of "bureaucratic insularity;" and (3) Large size and hierarchical structure causes "nonknowledgeability and nonparticipation of lower-level employees." Coase (1937, p. 341) calls these rationales "diminishing returns to management." The idea that the costs of management increase with size also implicitly follows from Alchian and Demsetz's analysis of the firm (1972). Their statement that "monitors are hired by the employees of the firm in order to reduce employee shirking" may be extended to the decreased ability of the monitor to effectively perform its function as the size of the firm (i.e., number of employees) increases. Therefore, the expected sign of this variable is negative in the VI equation, which means that larger firms will have smaller degree of vertical integration.

The sign will be positive in the FI equation with patents or R & D expenditure as a measure of FI, since the bigger the firm size the more the R & D output. This is because, as firm size increases, researchers become more productive by having more colleagues with whom to interact, and because knowledge production and its commercialization are more efficient by having the relevant complementary assets such as marketing, competitive manufacturing, and after-sales service within the firm's boundaries (Kamien and Schwartz, 1982; Teece, 1987). But FS's effect may be negative in the FI equation with R & D intensity as a measure of FI, because the difficulty of internal control of large firms may inhibit their R & D performance.

CASH is measured as the ratio of cash flow to sales.[12] We will use CASH, instead of the M-form structure (multidivisional firm structure) used by Levy (1985) and Teece (1980), as a measure of firm's managerial efficiency.

As Teece (1980) points out, while the M-form structure may enable firms to relax diseconomies associated with firm size by providing superior planning, coordination and control, the proposition that a firm with M-form structure is more efficient in management than other firms depends on firm size and firm-specific characteristics. M-form is needed only in response to increasingly complex administrative problems encountered as firm size and the diversity and magnitude of the firm's activities increase. Even if the variable CASH does not exclude nonmanagement phenomena such as market conditions, it serves as a better variable for managerial efficiency than M-form because greater cash flow in a firm reflects more internal funds for proceeding to vertical integration; this can be assured only by good management schemes and skills. Since we assume that good management schemes reduce the internalization cost of a firm, we expect that the sign of the variable CASH in the VI equation will be positive.

In the FI equation, the level of cash flow (LCASH) is expected to have a positive effect on FI, because cash flow reflects the internal funds available for R & D. The motivating assumption is that a firm invests its internal capital on R & D rather than external capital assuming that the internal cost of capital is below the external cost of capital. While a lag effect over several years was assumed in other literature because the capital budgeting decision takes time and because sustained changes in the firm's cash positions have more effect than one-year fluctuations (Armour and Teece, 1980), we will use only one year's data to avoid multicollinearity problem. For the same reason, the ratio of cash flow to sales (CASH) will also have a positive effect on FI when R & D intensity is used for FI.

In order to measure VAR, the past trend in sales is estimated for each firm. That is, the log of firm sales is regressed on a time trend. The variance of the deviation of sales from trend will then be used as a measure of the unanticipated variance in firm sales. The rationale for this variable for vertical integration was explained well in Bernhardt (1977). He said that suppliers adapt to demand fluctuations by adjusting price and other terms of sale, and by adjusting inventory, order backlog, or adjusting production rate. Vertical integration may reduce these adjustment costs by reducing actual variability as felt by individual suppliers and by increasing their knowledge of fluctuations through moving suppliers closer to final markets (Bernhardt, 1977, p. 214). However, there is the increasing risk of the obsolescence of the integrated production facility, because there is the high risk of a sudden decrease in demand for a final product. We assume that this risk will not be big enough to offset the positive effect, and thus we expect demand variability VAR to have a positive relationship with the level of vertical integration. All the variables with their expected signs are listed in Table 4.

The biggest problem in constructing the dataset was

Table 4: The Variables and Their Expected Signs

Variable	Definition	Expected Sign in FI Equation	Expected Sign in VI Equation
PAT	number of issued patents	NA	+
VI	degree of vertical integration	+	NA
CAP	ratio of capital to sales	+	+
LCAP	level of capital	+	NA
FS	firm size (total sales)	+/−	−
CASH	ratio of cash flow to sales	+	+
LCASH	level of cash flow	+	NA
VAR	unanticipated variance in firm sales	NA	+
R&D	level of R & D expenditure	+	+
RND	ratio of R & D expenditure to sales	+	+

encountered in patents data. To match relevant patents data with financial data, we managed the raw data as followings. First, since Standard and Poor's data are mainly constructed from 10-K's (a report taken from a firm's consolidated financial statements), each firm's relevant patent data should include those from both the parent company and its subsidiaries that are included in the consolidated financial statements. But patents data are reported individually for the parent company and for its subsidiaries, and not all of the subsidiaries are listed in some parent companies' 10-K's. Therefore, assuming that the unlisted subsidiaries' patents are not important, we count the number of patents of the parent company and the listed subsidiaries. Second, we count only the U.S. patents issued to each firm's overseas subsidiaries. Even if the overseas subsidiaries have patents in their countries and not in the U.S., we assume that the main outputs of their R & D activities are represented in the number of U.S. patents. Third, a special consideration is needed in the case of acquisition of a subsidiary during the sample years. If the subsidiary is acquired in 1974, its patent data for 1974 should not be included in the total number of the firm's patents for 1974. This is because the firm's financial data before 1974, which was used to construct R & D expenditure and environmental variables to match 1974 patent data, did not affect the subsidiary's 1974 patent data. Therefore, the patent data for acquired subsidiaries should be included in the firm's patent data one year after the acquisition.

All the variables of numerical amounts such as level of capital (LCAP), firm sales (FS), level of cash flow (LCASH), and R & D expenditure (R&D), are deflated by each year's producer price index of industrial commodities, because the deflated ones are the relevant absolute measure of the size variables. The means of the variables in the dataset can be found for different years in Table 5 and for different companies in Table 6.

Since at least one year's time lag is needed between environmental factors and issued patents, the variable PAT (issued patents) is of time $t + 1$ while all the other variables

Table 5: Means of Firm-Level Variables by Year, 1966-1986

YEAR	PAT	VI	LCAP	FS	LCASH	R&D	CAP	CASH	VAR	RND
66	.	.5624	25.4	140.3	10.74	9.90	.185	.081	.040	.069
67	42	.5356	48.3	283.5	19.46	15.62	.185	.074	.094	.057
68	66	.5393	52.5	336.0	22.00	9.80	.187	.068	.054	.055
69	82	.5411	60.7	374.4	24.55	10.31	.184	.066	.018	.056
70	78	.5285	62.6	370.3	23.77	10.61	.197	.060	.019	.046
71	92	.5075	62.1	361.6	21.73	10.00	.200	.062	.026	.042
72	60	.5148	64.4	399.0	23.55	13.22	.190	.066	.011	.040
73	53	.5350	73.4	448.0	28.39	15.81	.181	.067	.030	.039
74	59	.5086	67.7	428.8	26.55	14.55	.175	.066	.042	.036
75	51	.5043	58.8	365.3	22.32	10.81	.192	.060	.029	.037
76	52	.5076	67.0	417.5	27.96	13.37	.173	.074	.063	.037
77	51	.5094	70.5	452.9	33.20	15.06	.164	.078	.080	.037
78	52	.4949	89.0	503.8	36.83	17.60	.178	.078	.117	.037
79	40	.4991	98.1	513.3	40.05	18.29	.185	.077	.061	.037
80	44	.5192	104.2	531.3	36.52	22.26	.214	.066	.068	.042
81	41	.5182	104.5	529.1	39.24	25.49	.219	.071	.028	.048
82	51	.5480	106.3	506.1	37.50	27.45	.234	.063	.027	.051
83	59	.5208	113.5	523.9	34.39	33.30	.223	.068	.040	.056
84	74	.5534	130.6	576.9	52.96	37.37	.221	.080	.023	.055
85	.	.5194	143.3	580.9	46.56	42.16	.251	.071	.039	.061
86	.	.5053	.	.	.	.	.250	.079	.126	.061

Table 6: Means of Firm-Level Variables by Firm

Company Name	PAT	VI	LCAP	FS	LCASH	R&D	CAP	CASH	VAR	RND
Bell & Howell	58	.537	35.8	255	10.2	13.1	.14	.04	.004	.050
Conchemco Inc.	1	.302	4.4	37	1.1	.4	.15	.03	.257	.010
Sprague Elect.	33	.521	33.6	127	3.9	7.5	.26	.03	.021	.059
Crouse-Hinds	2	.540	14.4	99	8.2	1.5	.15	.08	.032	.014
Singer Co.	200	.535	188.0	1256	52.7	18.1	.15	.04	.033	.016
Gould Inc.	49	.473	126.0	500	30.3	26.0	.24	.06	.181	.046
AMP Inc.	118	.644	101.1	329	46.0	33.4	.31	.14	.063	.094
Rogers Corp.	3	.455	11.0	30	1.4	1.1	.37	.04	.012	.037
Thomas & Betts	22	.593	18.7	78	11.2	3.6	.25	.14	.011	.047
Texas Instrum.	161	.570	250.8	1085	109.7	69.1	.23	.10	.018	.055
Cutler-Hammer	24	.595	33.4	232	12.5	7.3	.16	.06	.014	.036
Raytheon Co.	83	.450	181.7	1467	79.7	39.3	.12	.05	.011	.026
Northern Telec.	56	.541	153.8	730	66.0	54.3	.20	.09	.008	.070
Thomas Indust.	2	.412	11.2	78	5.1	1.1	.15	.07	.015	.019
Acme Electric	25	.505	2.1	18	1.0	1.3	.12	.06	.013	.068

<u>Table 7</u>: Means and Pearson Product Moment Correlation
Coefficients

<u>Variable</u>	<u>N</u>	<u>Mean</u>	<u>Standard Deviation</u>
PAT	176	56.244	61.674
VI	166	.520	.089
LCAP	258	80.662	97.245
FS	259	439.063	525.791
LCASH	254	30.823	39.204
R&D	222	18.934	23.953
CAP	269	.199	.087
CASH	265	.070	.039
VAR	270	.049	.129
RND	232	.045	.027

Correlation Coefficients / Prob > |R| under H0: RHO = 0

	PAT	VI	LCAP	FS	LCASH	R&D	CAP	CASH	VAR	RND
PAT	1.000	.361	.772	.742	.745	.687	.039	.192	-.126	.226
	.000	.000	.000	.000	.000	.000	.613	.012	.099	.003
VI	.361	1.000	.153	-.009	.204	.250	.383	.695	-.503	.649
	.000	.000	.050	.906	.009	.002	.000	.000	.000	.000
LCAP	.772	.153	1.000	.910	.932	.879	.108	.151	-.057	.120
	.000	.050	.000	.000	.000	.000	.084	.016	.359	.075
FS	.742	-.009	.910	1.000	.865	.732	-.137	-.009	-.095	-.112
	.000	.906	.000	.000	.000	.000	.027	.882	.128	.097
LCASH	.745	.204	.932	.865	1.000	.887	.040	.309	-.104	.181
	.000	.009	.000	.000	.000	.000	.528	.000	.100	.007
R&D	.687	.250	.879	.732	.887	1.000	.137	.254	-.054	.392
	.000	.002	.000	.000	.000	.000	.041	.000	.425	.000
CAP	.039	.383	.108	-.137	.040	.137	1.000	.291	-.021	.427
	.613	.000	.084	.027	.528	.041	.000	.000	.727	.000
CASH	.192	.695	.151	-.009	.309	.254	.291	1.000	-.166	.423
	.012	.000	.016	.882	.000	.000	.000	.000	.007	.000
VAR	-.126	-.503	-.057	-.095	-.104	-.054	-.021	-.166	1.000	-.081
	.099	.000	.359	.128	.100	.425	.727	.007	.000	.220
RND	.226	.649	.120	-.112	.181	.392	.427	.423	-.081	1.000
	.003	.000	.075	.097	.007	.000	.000	.000	.220	.000

are of time t. Looking at the means for each firm's variables, we see that the size variables move in the same direction cross-sectionally. As a firm grows (i.e., FS rises), its other size variables (LCAP, LCASH, R&D) grow, too. But it is difficult to explain a variable's trend over time, because different companies have different years' data in the dataset. A Pearson product-moment correlation matrix for the variables can be found in Table 7.

The size variables including patents data are very dispersed while the ratio variables (VI, CAP, CASH, RND) are stable and are centered around means. We need to note that the correlation coefficients between each size variable and its ratio variable (LCAP and CAP, LCASH and CASH, R&D and RND) are not big (.108, .309, .392). This means that small firms with small amounts of capital and cash, and a small R & D budget may have high capital-intensity, a big cash ratio, and high R & D intensity. If the firm is very interested in innovation or very much involved in innovative activity, it will pour a large portion of its budget into R & D regardless of its size. This means that R & D intensity (RND) may be a better measure of R & D performance than the amount of R & D expenditure (R&D), because the former extracts the size effect at the stage of variable construction. It is clearly shown that the index of vertical integration (VI) is not correlated with the size variables of LCAP and FS (correlation coefficients are .153 and -.009). And it is more correlated with RND (.649) than R&D (.250). This supports the relevancy of RND rather than R&D to explain VI.

4.4 ESTIMATING THE EQUATION OF KNOWLEDGE PRODUCTION

The main hypothesis in our study is that the expectation of future innovation drives a firm to integrate vertically. As explained before, the legitimacy of the expection that vertical integration will enhance innovative performance needs to be tested first, before we go on to investigate the expectation's effect on vertical integration.

In our two-equation system, the second equation (FI equation) tests the hypothesis of vertical integration's positive effect on innovative performance. If one defines K as the level of economically valuable technological knowledge, $\dot{K}$ = dK/dt is the net accretion to it per unit of time. $\dot{K}$ is produced by a knowledge production function which translates past research expenditures into inventions. Firm-specific environmental factors affect the productivity of the knowledge production process inside the black box of innovative activity. As a measure of new invention $\dot{K}$ which is FI in our model, we use three different variables of number of issued patents (PAT), R & D expenditure (R&D), and R & D intensity (RND).

The model with patents as a dependent variable is

$$PAT = f \, (\, R\&D, \text{ firm-specific factors (VI, LCAP, FS, LCASH) }).$$

When R & D expenditure is used as a proxy of innovative output or performance, the environmental factors become the only independent variables to affect the productivity of the knowledge production process. We assume that the more productive firms with favorable environmental factors will devote more resources to R & D. Therefore, the model with R&D as a dependent variable is

$$R\&D = f \, (\text{ firm-specific factors (VI, LCAP, FS, LCASH) }).$$

In the same context, the model with RND as a dependent variable is

$$RND = f \, (\text{ firm-specific factors (VI, CAP, FS, CASH) }).$$

In all the equations of the following models, the error term is assumed to be identically and independently distributed with zero mean and constant variance, and therefore estimated through the Ordinary Least Squares (OLS) estimation method.

4.4.1 Patents as a Dependent Variable

When patents are used as a dependent variable, we do not include a lagged patent variable in the equation. The previous year's issued patents cannot be a proxy for a firm's technological endowment because each firm has a different patenting behavior.

As explained before, the time lag in a patent equation is either 1, 2, or 3. At first we will estimate the patent equation with a time lag of 1 year. That is, this year's number of patents issued is the function of the last year's firm-specific factors (VI, LCAP, FS, LCASH) and the previous three years' R & D expenditures. Regardless of the amount of time lag adopted between patents and the environmental factors, the previous three years' R & D expenditures are included in all the PAT equations. This is because we assume that a financial input will affect innovative activity over several years. So the first model is[13]

$$PAT_t = a_0 + a_1\ VI_{t-1} + a_2\ LCAP_{t-1} + a_3\ FS_{t-1} + a_4\ FS_{t-1}^2$$

$$+ a_5\ LCASH_{t-1} + a_6\ R\&D_{t-1} + a_7\ R\&D_{t-2} + a_8\ R\&D_{t-3}$$

$$+ u_t$$

where u_t is an error term.

If we impose two years' time lag between FI and VI, the relation will be

$$FI_t = f\ (\ VI_{t-1},\ VI_{t-2}\ ).[14]$$

In order to avoid any multicollinearity problem due to high correlation between the lagged values of a variable, we employ the time lag only on VI with the form of VI_{t-1} + VI_{t-2}. This additive form of VI will solve the problem of multicollinearity and short-term fluctuations in the measure of VI due to market conditions. The parameter of the additive form of VI will represent the effect of the previous years' VI on innovative activity. So the second model is

$$PAT_t = a_0 + a_1 (VI_{t-1} + VI_{t-2}) + a_2 LCAP_{t-1} + a_3 FS_{t-1}$$

$$+ a_4 FS_{t-1}^2 + a_5 LCASH_{t-1} + a_6 R\&D_{t-1} + a_7 R\&D_{t-2}$$

$$+ a_8 R\&D_{t-3} + u_t$$

In the same manner, the model with three years' time lag will be

$$PAT_t = a_0 + a_1 (VI_{t-1} + VI_{t-2} + VI_{t-3}) + a_2 LCAP_{t-1}$$

$$+ a_3 FS_{t-1} + a_4 FS_{t-1}^2 + a_5 LCASH_{t-1} + a_6 R\&D_{t-1}$$

$$+ a_7 R\&D_{t-2} + a_8 R\&D_{t-3} + u_t$$

Besides time lag problems, we encounter the question of whether we should use a dummy variable model or an error component model to treat firm-specific effect or time-specific effect in the empirical analysis of pooled time-series, cross-sectional data.

The basic equation in pooled time-series, cross-sectional data can be written as

$$Y = X b + u$$

where Y and u are n-vectors, X is a nk matrix of full rank

and b is a k vector of parameters to be estimated. The error term is broken into:

$$u_{it} = \alpha_i + \beta_t + e_{it}$$

where α_i and β_t are the systematic or specific effects associated with the ith firm and the tth year, respectively. Thus, it is recognized that Xb does not account for all the systematic variations in Y (Mundlak, 1978, p. 69).

A dummy variable model is a fixed effect model, which means that the firm-specific effect α_i or year-specific effect β_t is fixed rather than random. The fixed effect model does not make any specific assumptions about the distribution of α_i or β_t and thus the specific effects are represented in the different intercept by firm or year. The error component model is a random effect model, which means that α_i or β_t is random rather than fixed. In this case specific assumptions about the distribution of the specific effects are made. In the error component model the Generalized Least Squares (GLS) estimation method is used.

If the dummy variable model is true, the error component model has an omitted variable misspecifications, and its GLS estimator will be biased. If the error component model is correct, the dummy variable estimator will not be as efficient as the GLS estimator. Mundlak (1978) suggests that we use the dummy variable model if the specific effects and explanatory variables are correlated. When we use the dummy variable model, we can avoid specific assumptions about the population distribution. The error component model needs a rectangular form of data matrices for computer work. The traditional computational methods of error component model (e.g., the Fuller and Battes Method, the Parks Method, and the DaSilva Method) require the same number of years' data for each firm. But our dataset does not fit this requirement at all.

Given these considerations, we selected the following array of models to estimate.

1. the ordinary least squares model with no dummies (equation 1)

2. the least squares with year dummy variables model (equation 2)

3. the least squares with firm dummy variables model (equation 3)

4. the least squares with both year and firm dummy variables model (equation 4)

In equation 1 the intercept is constrained to a_0 for all firm-years. The other equations include firm and/or year dummy variables and thus allow the intercept to vary by firm and/or year. Under the assumption that each equation has the white noise error term, each equation is estimated with the OLS estimation method. Because we do not know which equation is a correct specification, we estimate all of them, and take an F-test to find out the correct one. As one of the equations is found to be a correct one, the estimator from all the other equations becomes a biased one.

But the dummy variable model which treats unobserved effects as fixed poses some problems relative to error component model. Inserting dummy variables to allow different intercepts across firms removes the firm-specific unobserved variation from the data, and the "effects" of the explanatory variables are estimated solely from the within-firm variation and is not influenced by the between-firm variation. Thus a fixed effects model would be liable to underestimate the parameters of independent variables.[15] In the same context, Maddala (1977, p. 328) indicates that the model with firm dummy variables often results in a loss of a large number of degrees of freedom and eliminates a large portion of the total variation if between-firm variation is large relative to within-firm variation.[16]

The estimation results are reported in Tables 8-10. The estimation results show that the value and sign of the parameter estimates significantly depend on the difference of model specification either with firm dummies or without firm dummies. That is, the degree of vertical integration makes a positive effect on the innovative output (issued patents) when firm dummy variables are not included, but does not positively effect it when firm dummy variables are included.

In order to answer the question of whether the model really needs to have firm dummy variables, we calculate the following F-statistic in terms of restricted and unrestricted residual sums of squares.[17] In the context of our hypotheses that

HO: all the parameters of firm dummy variables are zero
H1: the parameters are not all zero, the F-statistic is given
    by

$$F = \{(\,\bar{e}'\,\bar{e} - \hat{e}'\,\hat{e}\,) / (N - 1)\} / \{(\,\hat{e}'\,\hat{e}\,) / (NT - N - K)\}$$

where

1. $\bar{e}'\,\bar{e}$ is the restricted residual sum of squares from the model without firm dummy variables
2. $\hat{e}'\,\hat{e}$ is the unrestricted residual sum of squares from the model with firm dummy variables
3. $(N - 1)$ is the number of linear restrictions, i.e., the number of firm dummy variables
4. $(NT - N - K)$ is the number of degrees of freedom in the unrestricted model

If the calculated F-statistic is bigger than the critical F value with $[(N - 1), (NT - N - K)]$ degrees of freedom and a 1% significance level, we reject the null hypothesis and conclude that the intercepts of the firms are not all the same and thus the model with firm dummy variables is the one relevant to our study.

After we did the F-test for all the equations of the models with different time lags, we found that year dummy variables only minimally effected the model specification

Table 8: OLS Regression Model 1

$$PAT_t = f\,(\,VI_{t-1},\text{---})$$

(119 Observations)

Indep. Var.	Equation 1	Equation 2	Equation 3	Equation 4
c	-74.58*	28.29	-.65	68.72[d]
	(-4.06)	(.97)	(-.02)	(1.46)
VI_{t-1}	160.17*	120.33*	-4.35	-107.24
	(4.49)	(3.37)	(-.06)	(-1.22)
$LCAP_{t-1}$	.36*	.29*	-.14	-.0089
	(3.27)	(2.72)	(-1.23)	(-.07)
FS_{t-1}	.10*	.058[b]	11[d]	.089
	(3.99)	(2.15)	(1.60)	(1.26)
FS_{t-1}^2	-.000040*	-.000024[d]	-.000046[b]	-.000046[b]
	(-3.10)	(-1.76)	(-2.37)	(-2.48)
$LCASH_{t-1}$	-.30[d]	-.011	-.16	.15
	(-1.35)	(-.05)	(-.86)	(.76)
$R\&D_{t-1}$	-1.98*	-2.08*	-.30	-.69[d]
	(-3.47)	(-3.22)	(-.76)	(-1.57)
$R\&D_{t-2}$	.48	.82	1.01[b]	1.10[b]
	(.57)	(.95)	(2.08)	(2.21)
$R\&D_{t-3}$	1.79*	2.14*	.67[d]	.79[d]
	(2.88)	(3.40)	(1.61)	(1.78)
Year Dummy	No	Yes	No	Yes
Firm Dummy	No	No	Yes	Yes
R^2	.73	.80	.92	.94
F	38	17	53	38
D.W.	1.12	1.23	1.41	1.59

Note: t-statistics in parentheses

a indicates significant at the 1% level (two-tailed test)
b indicates significant at the 5% level (two-tailed test)
c indicates significant at the 10% level (two-tailed test)
d indicates significant at the 10% level (one-tailed test)

Table 9:   OLS Regression Model 2

$$PAT_t = f (VI_{t-1} + VI_{t-2}, \text{---})$$

(116 Observations)

Indep. Var.	Equation 1	Equation 2	Equation 3	Equation 4
C	-66.13[a]	-38.33[b]	4.29	32.63
	(-3.92)	(-2.04)	(.08)	(.63)
$VI_{t-1} + VI_{t-2}$	74.10[a]	56.60[a]	-7.25	-17.84
	(4.54)	(3.46)	(-.14)	(-.35)
$LCAP_{t-1}$	.25[b]	.23[b]	-.18[d]	-.087
	(2.48)	(2.43)	(-1.41)	(-.68)
FS_{t-1}	.060[b]	.023	.14[c]	.16[c]
	(2.52)	(.92)	(1.73)	(1.98)
FS_{t-1}^2	-.000017[d]	-.0000058	-.000045[b]	-.000045[b]
	(-1.45)	(-.45)	(-2.31)	(-2.43)
$LCASH_{t-1}$	-.25	-.061	-.22	-.056
	(-1.26)	(-.30)	(-1.11)	(-.28)
$R\&D_{t-1}$	-2.40[a]	-2.28[a]	-.48	-1.30[a]
	(-4.72)	(-3.95)	(-1.02)	(-2.65)
$R\&D_{t-2}$	1.32[c]	1.52[c]	1.09[b]	1.36[a]
	(1.75)	(1.95)	(2.18)	(2.70)
$R\&D_{t-3}$	2.12[a]	2.29[a]	.74[c]	.77[c]
	(3.84)	(4.05)	(1.72)	(1.79)
Year Dummy	No	Yes	No	Yes
Firm Dummy	No	No	Yes	Yes
R^2	.78	.83	.92	.94
F	47	22	46	37
D.W.	1.04	1.09	1.40	1.62

Note: t-statistics in parentheses

a indicates significant at the 1% level (two-tailed test)
b indicates significant at the 5% level (two-tailed test)
c indicates significant at the 10% level (two-tailed test)
d indicates significant at the 10% level (one-tailed test)

Table 10:   OLS Regression Model 3

$$PAT_t = f (VI_{t-1} + VI_{t-2} + VI_{t-3}, \text{---})$$

(112 Observations)

Indep. Var.	Equation 1	Equation 2	Equation 3	Equation 4
C	-70.19[a]	-44.44[b]	29.76	35.94
	(-4.02)	(-2.31)	(.48)	(.59)
$VI_{t-1} + VI_{t-2} + VI_{t-3}$	52.56[a]	41.97[a]	-21.40	-12.70
	(4.67)	(3.73)	(-.53)	(-.32)
$LCAP_{t-1}$	.29[a]	.25[b]	-.19[d]	-.056
	(2.80)	(2.54)	(-1.30)	(-.40)
FS_{t-1}	.062[b]	.028	.13[d]	.16[b]
	(2.61)	(1.08)	(1.64)	(2.02)
FS_{t-1}^2	-.000019[d]	-.0000075	-.000046[b]	-.000046[b]
	(-1.54)	(-.58)	(-2.28)	(-2.43)
$LCASH_{t-1}$	-.30[d]	-.090	-.19	-.073
	(-1.49)	(-.43)	(-.95)	(-.37)
$R\&D_{t-1}$	-2.24[a]	-2.26[a]	-.44	-1.38[a]
	(-4.37)	(-3.90)	(-.90)	(-2.65)
$R\&D_{t-2}$	.86	1.29[d]	1.15[b]	1.29[b]
	(1.09)	(1.60)	(2.12)	(2.40)
$R\&D_{t-3}$	2.22[a]	2.32[a]	.72[d]	.83[c]
	(3.99)	(4.10)	(1.61)	(1.85)
Year Dummy	No	Yes	No	Yes
Firm Dummy	No	No	Yes	Yes
R^2	.77	.82	.91	.93
F	44	20	41	34
D.W.	1.03	1.08	1.44	1.68

Note: t-statistics in parentheses

a indicates significant at the 1% level (two-tailed test)
b indicates significant at the 5% level (two-tailed test)
c indicates significant at the 10% level (two-tailed test)
d indicates significant at the 10% level (one-tailed test)

because the calculated F-statistic was very close to the critical value. But firm dummy variables were always very significant for the correct specification. Therefore, both equation 3 and equation 4 seem to be the suitable models. Thus we are forced to conclude that the empirical results with patents data do not support our hypothesis very well. Among the other explanatory variables, R & D expenditure after 2 and 3 years ($R\&D_{t-2}$, $R\&D_{t-3}$) consistently show a positive effect on issued patents regardless of the employed time lag between VI and FI. While the above result is what we expected, it is difficult to believe that $R\&D_{t-1}$ has a consistently negative sign.[18] LCAP has an insignificant negative sign, while FS has a significant positive sign. This may be due to the multicollinearity problem between LCAP and FS. LCASH also has an insignificant negative sign. Since innovative activity is a long-term project, it needs to be insulated from the day-to-day operation of a firm. Therefore, the relative financial independence of R & D from corporate operating divisions leads to the insignificant parameter value of LCASH in FI equation. The negative sign of squared FS means that the marginal productivity of firm size in innovative activity decreases as firm size increases.[19]

4.4.2 *R & D Expenditure (R&D) as a Dependent Variable*

The issued patents data is not a good measure of innovative output, simply because not all the firms apply patents for their innovative output and not all the ones applied for are approved. This is probably the biggest reason for our lack of good empirical results using patents data, the results which support our hypothesis that vertical integration helps innovative activity through knowledge complementarity effect. The second reason related to this is that, since between-firm variation of patent data is very large relative to within-firm variation, firm dummy variables seem to eliminate a big portion of the total variation so that

VI's parameter with firm dummies becomes insignificant. In this regard, R & D expenditure data can be a useful proxy for innovative output. That is, with R & D expenditure data we neither have the big problem of managing patent data such as attempting to match subsidiaries and parent companies, nor do we need to assume time lag between the application for and issuance of patents. The between-firm variation of R&D is not large compared to patents data.[20] A lagged R&D variable is included in the equation as an explanatory variable. It is a useful proxy for a firm's technological endowment.

The time lag in the R&D equation is one year short compared to the case of issued patents, since there is no time consumed between application and issuance. Thus we adopt the time lag of either 0, 1, or 2 years between VI and R&D. With no time lag the model is

$$R\&D_t = a_0 + a_1 R\&D_{t-1} + a_2 VI_t + a_3 LCAP_t + a_4 FS_t$$
$$+ a_5 FS_t^2 + a_6 LCASHt + u_t$$

where u_t is an error term. With time lag of 1, the model is

$$R\&D_t = a_0 + a_1 R\&D_{t-1} + a_2 (VI_t + VI_{t-1}) + a_3 LCAP_t$$
$$+ a_4 FS_t + a_5 FS_t^2 + a_6 LCASH_t + u_t$$

With time lag of 2, the model is

$$R\&D_t = a_0 + a_1 R\&D_{t-1} + a_2 (VI_t + VI_{t-1} + VI_{t-2})$$
$$+ a_3 LCAP_t + a_4 FS_t + a_5 FS_t^2 + a_6 LCASH_t + u_t$$

The estimation results are reported in Tables 11-13.

Table 11: OLS Regression Model 4

$$R\&D_t = f (VI_t, ---)$$

(141 Observations)

Indep. Var.	Equation 1	Equation 2	Equation 3	Equation 4
C	2.52	4.23	-7.48	-5.90
	(0.82)	(1.14)	(-.77)	(-.53)
R&D$_{t-1}$	.93*	.84*	.78*	.71*
	(18.29)	(14.87)	(12.15)	(9.21)
VI$_t$	-6.77	-6.18	13.54	14.85
	(-1.14)	(-1.05)	(.71)	(.71)
LCAP$_t$	.045	.026^d	.052^b	.034
	(2.74)	(1.65)	(2.03)	(1.21)
FS$_t$	-.0017	.0037	.041*	.037^b
	(-.46)	(.93)	(2.72)	(2.34)
FS$_t^2$	-.0000020	-.0000044^b	-.000014*	-.000012*
	(-1.11)	(-2.29)	(-3.53)	(-3.03)
LCASH$_t$	.057^d	.098*	.060^d	.11^b
	(1.60)	(2.66)	(1.35)	(2.27)
Year Dummy	No	Yes	No	Yes
Firm Dummy	No	No	Yes	Yes
R^2	.96	.97	.97	.98
F	512	152	194	124
D.W.	1.68	1.53	2.03	1.87

Note: t-statistics in parentheses

a indicates significant at the 1% level (two-tailed test)
b indicates significant at the 5% level (two-tailed test)
c indicates significant at the 10% level (two-tailed test)
d indicates significant at the 10% level (one-tailed test)

Table 12: OLS Regression Model 5

$$R\&D_t = f(\ VI_t + VI_{t-1},---)$$

(136 Observations)

Indep. Var.	Equation 1	Equation 2	Equation 3	Equation 4
c	3.06	2.88	-17.40^c	-21.82^b
	(.97)	(.76)	(-1.81)	(-2.05)
R&D$_{t-1}$	.97^a	.87^a	.73^a	.64^a
	(17.96)	(14.06)	(12.82)	(9.52)
VI$_t$ + VI$_{t-1}$	-3.77	-2.86	16.44^c	23.16^b
	(-1.23)	(-.94)	(1.74)	(2.30)
LCAP$_t$	.044^b	.027^d	.026	.0059
	(2.58)	(1.65)	(1.04)	(.22)
FS$_t$	-.0038	.0022	.061^a	.063^a
	(-1.00)	(.53)	(4.44)	(4.43)
FS$_t^2$	-.00000094	-.0000034^c	-.000011^a	-.0000098^a
	(-.50)	(-1.71)	(-3.18)	(-3.02)
LCASH$_t$	.043	.079^b	-.041	-.0081
	(1.22)	(2.13)	(-1.04)	(-.20)
Year Dummy	No	Yes	No	Yes
Firm Dummy	No	No	Yes	Yes
R^2	.96	.97	.98	.98
F	503	147	256	167
D.W.	1.63	1.50	1.79	1.73

Note: t-statistics in parentheses

a indicates significant at the 1% level (two-tailed test)
b indicates significant at the 5% level (two-tailed test)
c indicates significant at the 10% level (two-tailed test)
d indicates significant at the 10% level (one-tailed test)

Table 13: OLS Regression Model 6

$$R\&D_t = f (VI_t + VI_{t-1} + VI_{t-2}, \cdots)$$

(125 Observations)

Indep. Var.	Equation 1	Equation 2	Equation 3	Equation 4
c	3.89 (1.16)	3.48 (.87)	-22.43^c (-1.86)	-33.70^b (-2.57)
$R\&D_{t-1}$	.99^a (17.40)	.90^a (13.40)	.69^a (10.56)	.56^a (7.27)
$VI_t + VI_{t-1} + VI_{t-2}$	-3.11^d (-1.44)	-2.23 (-1.03)	14.23^c (1.80)	23.22^a (2.78)
$LCAP_t$	.038^b (2.09)	.024^d (1.32)	.018 (.61)	.0059 (.20)
FS_t	-.0043 (1.05)	.0014 (.31)	.070^a (4.73)	.068^a (4.56)
FS_t^2	-.00000087 (-.44)	-.0000031^d (-1.46)	-.000011^a (-3.14)	-.0000092^a (-2.74)
$LCASH_t$	.052^d (1.42)	.084^b (2.17)	-.056^d (-1.40)	-.026 (-.62)
Year Dummy	No	Yes	No	Yes
Firm Dummy	No	No	Yes	Yes
R^2	.96	.97	.98	.98
F	459	138	238	165
D.W.	1.93	1.79	1.68	1.60

Note: t-statistics in parentheses

a indicates significant at the 1% level (two-tailed test)
b indicates significant at the 5% level (two-tailed test)
c indicates significant at the 10% level (two-tailed test)
d indicates significant at the 10% level (one-tailed test)

Regardless of the number of employed time lags, the estimation results from the R&D equation consistently show the same pattern. While VI's parameter was insignificant in the equation without firm dummies (equation 1 and 2), it was mostly significantly positive in the equation with firm dummies (equation 3 and 4). The VI's significance increases as we use the sum of several years' VI with the time lags, because the added value or the moving average of several successive years is more stable than the one-year value. Since we found that firm dummies were essential and year dummies were unnecessary (although their calculated F-statistics are pretty close to one another as compared to the case of patents), we believe that the estimation results with R & D expenditure data support our hypothesis. In equations 3 and 4 of Tables 12 and 13, we found that vertical integration positively and significantly affects innovative activity, although the effect was insignificant in Table 11. The significance increases as the additive sum of more years' VI is used. The sign of the lagged R&D variable is significantly positive to show the effect of technological endowment on innovative activity. The size variables of LCAP and FS have mostly positive signs as we expected. But LCASH shows some mixed signs. Again, this is because of the relative independence of R&D from corporate operating divisions for financial support. The negative sign of squared FS means that the marginal productivity of firm size in innovative activity decreases as the firm size increases.

4.4.3   R & D Intensity (RND) as a Dependent Variable

Different specifications in PAT and R&D equations, especially when including or excluding firm dummies, produced very different parameter values and significance. While firm-size effects were considered at the stage of estimation in those equations, R & D intensity is the variable normalized by the size effects (sales) at the time of variable construction. The relevancy of this ratio variable as compared to the size variables of PAT and R&D is presented in the previous chapter (p. 52). The relevant hypothesis is that more vertically integrated firms, even if they are only small firms, will have more intensive R & D propensity than less vertically integrated firms. Although RND is the variable which is affected by sales as well as R & D expenditure,[21] it is a good proxy for innovative output under the assumption that a firm keeps its portion of the R & D budget, not the absolute amount of R & D expenditure, constant as it expects no change in R & D productivity. Since a ratio variable (VI) explains another ratio variable (RND) both of which are very stable, we expect consistent estimation results for all the explanatory variables regardless of specification difference.

The independent variable FS on the right-hand-side of the RND equation will have a different meaning from the previous one. In PAT and R&D equations, FS was assumed to have a positive sign, because bigger firms generally produce more R & D output than smaller firms. But in the RND equation it may have negative sign, since big firms are assumed to have a less efficient management and thus may be less productive in R & D. The managerial inefficiency of big firms is implied by the negative sign of squared FS in PAT and R&D equations. Since RND is already normalized by FS, the variable FS^2 will not be included in the RND equation. The ratio variables of capital intensity (CAP) and cash ratio (CASH) are used to explain RND, and they are expected to have positive effects. Since we consistently got the same result regardless of the employed number of time lags in PAT and R&D equations, we will use only two different time lags of either 0 or 1 in the RND equation. The model with no time lag will be

$$RND_t = a_0 + a_1 RND_{t-1} + a_2 VI_t + a_3 CAP_t + a_4 FS_t$$

$$+ a_5 CASH_t + u_t$$

where u_t is an error term. With time lag 1 the model will be

$$RND_t = a_0 + a_1 RND_{t-1} + a_2 (VI_t + VI_{t-1}) + a_3 CAP_t$$

$$+ a_4 FS_t + a_5 CASH_t + u_t$$

The estimation results are reported in Tables 14-15.

After we took F-tests for the RND models' dummy variables, we found that equations 2 and 3 in $RND_t = f(VI_t)$ and $RND_t = f(VI_t + VI_{t-1})$ were good specifications. The empirical results with these equations strongly support our hypothesis that the degree of vertical integration (VI) positively affects R & D intensity (RND). CAP and FS appeared to be significantly positive, but CASH had a mostly negative and insignificant sign. Both the variable LCASH in the PAT and R&D equations and the variable CASH in the RND equation are shown to have no consistent positive effect on innovative output. The reason stems from the fact that R & D financing is insulated from corporate operating divisions in most firms and thus the cash portion of operating divisions is not directly related to the innovative activity. The lagged RND variable has a very significant positive sign as a proxy for technological endowment. In the next chapter we will examine the determinants of vertical integration in the equation with expected R & D output.

4.5 ESTIMATING THE EQUATION OF VERTICAL INTEGRATION

This chapter is devoted to estimating the main hypothesis: the more a firm intends to innovate in the future, the more the firm vertically integrates today (because using external market for innovation like contract R & D or technology licensing incurs big transaction costs).

The previous literature (Armour and Teece, 1980) on

<u>Table 14</u>:   OLS Regression Model 7

$$RND_t = f\ (\ VI_t,\ \text{---}\ )$$

(142 Observations)

Indep. Var.	Equation 1	Equation 2	Equation 3	Equation 4
C	-.0032	-.0071^c	-.011	-.027^a
	(-.87)	(-1.78)	(-1.03)	(-3.05)
RND$_{t-1}$	.94^a	.89^a	.71^a	.76^a
	(35.77)	(32.01)	(12.20)	(15.00)
VI$_t$	.0045	.020^b	.052^b	.093^a
	(.49)	(2.14)	(2.29)	(4.13)
CAP$_t$	.011^d	.0099^d	.048^a	.020
	(1.58)	(1.42)	(3.19)	(1.23)
FS$_t$	-.0000016^c	-.000000020	-.0000071^c	-.000068^c
	(1.75)	(-.02)	(1.96)	(1.68)
CASH$_t$	.0049	-.014	-.060^d	-.10^b
	(.29)	(-.79)	(-1.48)	(-2.53)
Year Dummy	No	Yes	No	Yes
Firm Dummy	No	No	Yes	Yes
R^2	.95	.96	.96	.97
F	502	140	164	105
D.W.	1.94	2.03	1.93	2.13

Note: t-statistics in parentheses

a indicates significant at the 1% level (two-tailed test)
b indicates significant at the 5% level (two-tailed test)
c indicates significant at the 10% level (two-tailed test)
d indicates significant at the 10% level (one-tailed test)

Table 15: OLS Regression Model 8

$$RND_t = f (VI_t + VI_{t-1}, ---)$$

(136 Observations)

Indep. Var.	Equation 1	Equation 2	Equation 3	Equation 4
c	-.0022	-.0044	-.011	-.026[b]
	(-.58)	(-1.06)	(-.93)	(-2.44)
RND_{t-1}	.94[a]	.89[a]	.68[a]	.74[a]
	(34.12)	(30.36)	(10.95)	(13.03)
$VI_t + VI_{t-1}$	.00064	.0076[d]	.027[b]	.044[a]
	(.13)	(1.54)	(2.06)	(3.26)
CAP_t	.011[d]	.010[d]	.047[a]	.024[d]
	(1.59)	(1.47)	(3.01)	(1.49)
FS_t	-.0000015[d]	-.000000011	-.000010[b]	-.0000080[c]
	(1.60)	(-.01)	(2.47)	(1.69)
$CASH_t$	.018	.0043	-.047	-.059[d]
	(1.05)	(.25)	(-1.18)	(-1.43)
Year Dummy	No	Yes	No	Yes
Firm Dummy	No	No	Yes	Yes
R^2	.95	.96	.96	.97
F	491	141	162	103
D.W.	1.93	2.03	1.90	2.16

Note: t-statistics in parentheses

a indicates significant at the 1% level (two-tailed test)
b indicates significant at the 5% level (two-tailed test)
c indicates significant at the 10% level (two-tailed test)
d indicates significant at the 10% level (one-tailed test)

this subject examined only the FI equation which represents a technological relationship, in order to support the hypothesis that firms integrate vertically to help their R & D activity. In our study we estimate the VI equation (behavioral relationship) directly to test the transaction cost hypothesis. Since the expectation that vertical integration would enhance innovative performance was supported by our empirical results from the FI equation, the VI equation is ready to have an expected R & D output as an independent variable. No past research on vertical integration has considered an expectation variable as a determinant of vertical integration. We will introduce here a new two-equation model, in which an expectation variable appears in the behavioral equation VI, and the technological equation FI makes the VI equation estimable by solving the econometric problems related to the expectation variable. Although the assumed time lags were either 0, 1, or 2, we will adopt only 0 or 1 time lag to avoid computational complications. That is, the model will be

$$VI_t = f(E_t(FI_t)) \text{ and } FI_t = g(VI_t)$$

or

$$VI_t = f(E_t(FI_{t+1})) \text{ and } FI_{t+1} = g(VI_t)$$

Since we assume that all the variables including R & D output are observable at time t, $E_t(FI_t)$ is just a realized value FI_t. We will not use patents data in estimating the VI equation, because the estimation results of the FI equation demonstrated that patents data was not a good proxy for innovative output. The first model with no time lag and R&D as FI will be the two equations

$$VI_t = a_0 + a_1 VI_{t-1} + a_2 R\&D_t + a_3 CAP_t + a_4 FS_t$$

$$+ a_5 CASH_t + a_6 VAR + a_7 TD + a_8 FD + u_t$$

and

$$R\&D_t = b_0 + b_1 R\&D_{t-1} + b_2 VI_t + b_3 LCAP_t + b_4 FS_t$$
$$+ b_5 FS_t + b_6 LCASH_t + b_7 TD + b_8 FD + \eta_t$$

where u_t and η_t are error terms. TD and FD are the vectors of year and time dummy variables, and a_7, a_8, b_7, and b_8 are the vectors of their parameters. Both equations are overidentified. The second model with no time lag and RND as FI will be the two equations

$$VI_t = a_0 + a_1 VI_{t-1} + a_2 RND_t + a_3 CAP_t + a_4 FS_t$$
$$+ a_5 CASH_t + a_6 VAR + a_7 TD + a_8 FD + u_t$$

and

$$RND_t = b_0 + b_1 RND_{t-1} + b_2 VI_t + b_3 CAP_t + b_4 FS_t$$
$$+ b_5 CASH_t + b_6 TD + b_7 FD + \eta_t$$

The VI equation is exactly identified and the RND equation is overidentified. These two models are simple simultaneous equation models because the two endogenous variables (VI and FI) affect one another at the same time t. Therefore, they will be estimated by the 2SLS method.

The third model with time lag 1 and RND as FI will be the two equations of

$$(1)\ VI_t = a_1 VI_{t-1} + a_2 E_t (RND_{t+1}) + a_3 CAP_t + a_4 FS_t$$
$$+ a_5 CASH_t + a_6 VAR_t + a_7 TD + a_8 FD + u_t$$

and

$$(2)\ RND_{t+1} = b_1\ RND_t + b_2\ VI_t + b_3\ CAP_t + b_4\ FS_t$$

$$+\ b_5\ CASH_t + b_6\ TD + b_7\ FD + \eta_{t+1}$$

where u_t and η_{t+1} are disturbances with mean zero, TD and FD are the vectors of year and time dummy variables, and a_7, a_8, b_6, and b_7 are the vectors of their parameters.

This is a dynamic simultaneous equation model with lagged variables. In estimating this model, we encounter two prominent problems. First, the expectation variable $E_t(RND_{t+1})$ is unobservable at time t. Second, $E_t(RND_{t+1})$ is correlated with the disturbance term u_t, because

$$(3)\ E_t\ (RND_{t+1}) = b_1\ RND_t + b_2\ VI_t + b_3\ CAP_t + b_4\ FS_t$$

$$+\ b_5\ CASH_t + b_6\ TD + b_7\ FD$$

when we take an expectation on equation (2) at time t. That is, u_t affects VI_t in equation (1), VI_t affects $E_t(RND_{t+1})$ in equation (3), and thus u_t is correlated with $E_t(RND_{t+1})$ But η_{t+1} is not correlated with the independent variable VI_t in equation (2), because η_{t+1} affects RND_{t+1}, not $E_t(RND_{t+1})$. Therefore, we can estimate equation (2) with the simple OLS method. This means that the two equation model is a recursive model.

To solve the problems in estimating equation (1), we construct the expectation variable $E_t(RND_{t+1})$ as a function of all the current and past variables which are observable at time t. If we substitute (1) into (2), we get

$$(4)\ RND_{t+1} = b_1\ RND_t + b_2\ \{\ a_1\ VI_{t-1} + a_2\ E_t\ (RND_{t+1})$$

$$+\ a_3\ CAP_t + a_4\ FS_t + a_5\ CASH_t + a_6\ VAR_t$$

$$+ a_7 \, TD + a_8 \, FD + u_t \} + b_3 \, CAP_t + b_4 \, FS_t$$

$$+ b_5 \, CASH_t + b_6 \, TD + b_7 \, FD + \eta_{t+1}$$

If we take expectations on both sides at time t assuming E_t $\{ (b_2 \, u_t + \eta_{t+1})| \, I_t \} = 0$, where I_t is the information set at time t, we get $E_t(RND_{t+1})$ as a function of observable variables. It becomes

(5) $E_t(RND_{t+1}) = \{ b_1 / (1 - b_2 a_2) \} \, RND_t + \{ (b_2 a_1)$

$/ (1 - b_2 a_2) \} \, VI_{t-1} + \{ (b_3 + b_2 a_3) / (1 - b_2 a_2) \}$

$CAP_t + \{ (b_4 + b_2 a_4) / (1 - b_2 a_2) \} \, FS_t + \{ (b_5 + b_2 a_5)$

$/ (1 - b_2 a_2) \} \, CASH_t + \{ (b_2 a_6) / (1 - b_2 a_2) \} \, VAR_t$

$+ \{ (b_6 + b_2 a_7) / (1 - b_2 a_2) \} \, TD + \{ (b_7 + b_2 a_8)$

$/ (1 - b_2 a_2) \} \, FD$

If we substitute (5) into (1), we get

(6) $VI_t = a_1 \, VI_{t-1} + a_2 \, [\, \{ b_1 / (1 - b_2 a_2) \} \, RND_t + \{ (b_2 a_1)$

$/ (1 - b_2 a_2) \} \, VI_{t-1} + \{ (b_3 + b_2 a_3) / (1 - b_2 a_2) \}$

$CAP_t + \{ (b_4 + b_2 a_4) / (1 - b_2 a_2) \} \, FS_t + \{ (b_5$

$+ b_2 a_5) / (1 - b_2 a_2) \} \, CASH_t + \{ (b_2 a_6) / (1 - b_2 a_2) \}$

$VAR_t + \{ (b_6 + b_2 a_7) / (1 - b_2 a_2) \} \, TD + \{ (b_7$

$+ b_2 a_8) / (1 - b_2 a_2) \} \, FD \,] + a_3 \, CAP_t + a_4 \, FS_t$

$+ a_5 \, CASH_t + a_6 \, VAR_t + a_7 \, TD + a_8 \, FD + u_t$

And thus

$$(7)\ VI_t = \{\ a_1\ /\ (1 - b_2 a_2)\ \}\ VI_{t-1} + \{\ (b_1 a_2)\ /\ (1 - b_2 a_2)\ \}\ RND_t$$

$$+ \{\ (a_3 + b_3 a_2)\ /\ (1 - b_2 a_2)\ \}\ CAP_t + \{\ (a_4 + b_4 a_2)$$

$$/\ (1 - b_2 a_2)\ \}\ FS_t + \{\ (a_5 + b_5 a_2)\ /\ (1 - b_2 a_2)\ \}\ CASH_t$$

$$+ \{\ a_6\ /\ (1 - b_2 a_2)\ \}\ VAR_t + \{\ (a_7 + b_6 a_2)\ /\ (1$$

$$-\ b_2 a_2)\ \}\ TD + \{\ (a_8 + b_7 a_2)\ /\ (1 - b_2 a_2)\ \}\ FD + u_t$$

Equation (7) is the reduced form of equation (1), i.e., it is the function of all the predetermined variables. Equation (2) and equation (7) are the ones to be actually estimated. No explanatory variable in those equations is correlated with the disturbance term u_t or η_{t+1}. We use a nonlinear estimation method to get the estimates of the structural parameters which are restricted across the reduced-form equations. Because both equation (2) and equation (7) are free from any correlation problem between explanatory variables and disturbance term, they can be estimated through SYSNLIN OLS in SAS program. The SYSNLIN OLS program minimizes iteratively the sum of squares of the error terms starting from certain parameter values until the sum of squares converge to a certain level. The Gauss method is used as a minimization method to produce the estimates of the structural parameters.

The fourth model with time lag 1 and R&D as FI will be

$$(8)\ VI_t = a_1\ VI_{t-1} + a_2\ E_t(R\&D_{t+1}) + a_3\ CAP_t + a_4\ FS_t$$

$$+ a_5\ CASH_t + a_6\ VAR_t + a_7\ TD + a_8\ FD + u_t$$

and

(9) $R\&D_{t+1} = b_1 R\&D_t + b_2 VI_t + b_3 LCAP_t + b_4 FS_t$

$\qquad + b_5 FS_t^2 + b_6 LCASH_t + b_7 TD + b_8 FD + \eta_{t+1}$

Equation (9) can be estimated by OLS. Equation (8), however, has the same problems as equation (1), such as the unobservable expectation variable and the correlation between the independent variable and error term. After we follow the same steps as before, we get the following equation

(10) $VI_t = \{ a_1 / (1 - b_2 a_2) \} VI_{t-1} + \{ (a_2 b_1) / (1 - b_2 a_2) \}$

$\qquad R\&D_t + \{ a_3 / (1 - b_2 a_2) \} CAP_t + \{ (a_2 b_3) / (1$

$\qquad - b_2 a_2) \} LCAP_t + \{ (a_4 + b_4 a_2) / (1 - b_2 a_2) \} FS_t$

$\qquad + \{ (b_5 a_2) / (1 - b_2 a_2) \} FS_t^2 + \{ a_5 / (1 - b_2 a_2) \}$

$\qquad CASH_t + \{ (a_2 b_6) / (1 - b_2 a_2) \} LCASH_t + \{ a_6 / (1$

$\qquad - b_2 a_2) \} VAR_t + \{ (a_7 + b_7 a_2) / (1 - b_2 a_2) \} TD$

$\qquad + \{ (a_8 + b_8 a_2) / (1 - b_2 a_2) \} FD + u_t$

Equations (9) and (10) will be estimated through the SYSNLIN OLS program as before. The estimation results are reported in Tables 16-18.

The estimation results from the models with RND as FI support our main hypothesis very well. Expected future innovation, regardless of the number of employed time lags, significantly (mostly at the .01 significance level) influences today's vertical integration. In the models with R&D as FI, expected future innovation has an insignificant positive effect on vertical integration. Since the ratio variable RND is a good proxy for the expected return on R & D and is

<u>Table 16</u>:   2SLS Regression Models

Independent Variables	$VI_t = f (RND_t, ---)$ (136 Observations)	$VI_t = f (R\&D_t, ---)$ (136 Observations)
c	.19[a] (5.43)	.25[a] (5.74)
VI_{t-1}	.34[a] (4.05)	.36[a] (4.24)
$R\&D_t$	–	.00047 (1.06)
RND_t	1.00[a] (4.28)	–
CAP_t	.12[b] (2.28)	.21[a] (3.32)
FS_t	-.000045[a] (-2.67)	-.000041 (-1.28)
$CASH_t$	.98[a] (7.27)	.95[a] (7.04)
VAR_t	-.030 (1.24)	.010 (1.22)
R^2	.97	.97
F	93	92
D.W.	1.91	1.96

Note: 1. t-statistics in parentheses
         2. Both equations include year and firm dummies

a indicates significant at the 1% level (two-tailed test)
b indicates significant at the 5% level (two-tailed test)
d indicates significant at the 10% level (one-tailed test)

Table 17:   SYSNLIN OLS Regression 1

(138 Observations)

Independent Variables	$VI_t = f \{E_t (RND_{t,i})\}$	$RND_{t,i} = g (VI_t)$
VI_{t-1}	.30[a] (3.57)	—
$E_t(RND_{t,i})$	1.20[a] (2.95)	—
RND_t	—	.67[a] (9.57)
VI_t	—	.023 (.93)
CAP_t	.17[b] (2.60)	−.018 (−1.09)
FS_t	−.000056[a] (−2.79)	.000011[b] (2.38)
$CASH_t$	.89[a] (5.72)	.072 (1.60)
VAR_t	.0020 (.08)	—
R^2	.97	.97

Note: 1. t-statistics in parentheses
2. Both equations include year and firm dummies

a indicates significant at the 1% level (two-tailed test)
b indicates significant at the 5% level (two-tailed test)

<u>Table 18:</u>   SYSNLIN OLS Regression 2

(134 Observations)

Independent Variables	$VI_t = f \{ E_t (R\&D_{t+1}) \}$	$R\&D_{t+1} = g (VI_t)$
VI_{t+1}	.31[*] (3.38)	—
$E_t(R\&D_{t+1})$	.00058[d] (1.38)	—
$R\&D_t$	—	.81[*] (8.49)
VI_t	—	48.02[b] (2.09)
CAP_t	.20[*] (2.74)	—
$LCAP_t$	—	.10[*] (2.97)
FS_t	-.000051[d] (-1.54)	.012 (.62)
FS_t^2	—	-.0000027 (-.64)
$CASH_t$	.89[*] (5.73)	—
$LCASH_t$	—	-.13[b] (-2.45)
VAR_t	.0086 (.34)	—
R^2	.97	.98

Note: 1. t-statistics in parentheses
       2. Both equations include year and firm dummies

a indicates significant at the 1% level (two-tailed test)
b indicates significant at the 5% level (two-tailed test)
d indicates significant at the 10% level (one-tailed test)

very stable compared to the amount variable R&D, we can believe that our hypothesis is empirically supported very well. That is, expected future innovation is an important determinant of vertical integration (through transaction costs).[22]

We tested the stability condition of the dynamic simultaneous equation model with the estimated parameters of E(FI) in the VI equation and VI in the FI equation. When FI = RND, the estimated parameter value of E(RND) in the VI equation is 1.20. The estimated parameter value of VI in the RND equation is .023. Since $1 / 1.20 > .023$, the model satisfies the stability condition. In the same way, the model with R&D as FI was also found to satisfy the stability condition.

The relationship between vertical integration and capital intensity is consistently positive over all the equations as expected (mostly at the .01 significance level). Since capital generally refers to a firm's immobile resources, as capital intensity increases the firm's asset specificity increases, too. Since vertical integration saves transaction costs due to the asset specificity, capital intensity has a positive relationship with vertical integration. Firm size has a negative sign in all the equations mostly at the .05 significance level, as expected. This is consistent with the argument that as firm size increases internalization costs rise, and thus vertical integration decreases. The ratio of cash flow to sales has a very significant positive relationship with vertical integration (at the .01 significance level). This is consistent with the argument that, because a high cash flow ratio may represent managerial efficiency of a firm and good management reduces the internalization cost, high cash flow ratio leads to high vertical integration. But the variable of unexpected change in firm demand has a very insignificant effect on vertical integration. The reason seems to be that the increasing risk of fluctuating demands makes the firm hesitate in the expansion of its business. The lagged VI variable has a very significant positive effect on VI (at the .01 significance level) to show partial adjustment of vertical integration.

4.6 SUMMARY, LIMITATIONS, AND SUGGESTED FURTHER RESEARCH

The purpose of this study was to examine the relationship between vertical integration and the innovative activity of a firm. Compared to the previous literature, this study, in particular, examined the effect of a firm's expectation about future innovation on vertical integration. The empirical results supported our hypotheses very well. The empirical results of the knowledge production function showed that vertical integration provides a good firm-specific environment for innovative activity. The empirical results of the vertical integration equation supported our main hypothesis that the more a firm intends to innovate in the future, the more the firm vertically integrates today. But this study has some empirical limitations.

First of all our biggest problem was in getting the data needed to construct the measure of vertical integration. With only 15 firms in our sample it was difficult to generalize our empirical findings. The second problem that we encountered was in setting the number of time lags between vertical integration and future innovation. Although we employed some specific years in each model (1-3 years in the PAT equation and 0-2 years in the R&D equation) commonly for all the years and all the sample firms, we should have adopted different time lag for each firm and for each year. The third problem, and the one we think remains fairly ambiguous, stems from our not finding any saturation or threshold effect of vertical integration on future innovation. The semi-log functional form did not give better empirical results than the simple linear model. It simply did not fit the data observations better than others.

We suggest that future studies focus on the expansion of the dataset, on refining the time lags, on trying different functional forms for different groups of data, on finding better proxies for innovational performance, and on using different measures of vertical integration.

We also suggest that the relationship between vertical integration and R & D activity be investigated in more detail than occurred in this study. The relationship depends on the degree of linkage between the research staff and operating personnel. In some firms, R & D division is separate, and has its own long-term mission. In other firms, R & D organization is consolidated with other types of technical support to make the total R & D effort more accessible and more responsive to the operating organizations. Besides the pure degree of vertical integration, these specific managerial or organizational behavior of a firm, which can either amplify or nullify the effect of vertical integration on innovative activity, needs to be investigated further.

Notes

1. For the study of knowledge complementarity between divisions within a firm, SBU may be a better unit of analysis than a firm. With SBU as a unit of analysis, knowledge complementarity may represent R & D spillovers between divisions.

2. This is shown by its relatively high average ratio of R & D expenditure to sales (0.046 in our sample firms) compared to other industries.

3. Eleven occurrences of missing values were found for all the variables in the dataset.

4. To correct for a missing value after only one year's observation, we calculated the percentage growth over the following two years and multiplied its inverse times the value of the variable for the first following year.

5. While Levy (1981) used this method for the dependent variable VI, we will use it only for the independent variable VI. When an additive sum of a variable and its lagged ones is used as a dependent variable, it creates a problem in adopting the number of time lag between dependent and independent variables.

6. Labor and related expense includes salaries, wages, pension costs, profit sharing and incentive compensation, payroll taxes and other employee benefits (Compustat Manual, 4/15/1986, section 8, p. 62).

7. Usually only chemical formulas and industrial-commercial processes (for example, cosmetics and recipes) can be protected as trade secrets after they are placed on the market.

8. The demand curve for an input is given by the input price equal to the value of marginal product of the input (r = VMP = p MP). Under the assumption of given prices p and r, the demand for the input increases as its marginal product increases. Therefore, if vertical integration increases marginal productivity of R & D, vertical integration will be directly related to R & D expenditure.

9. A sample of the time lag between patent application and issuance is presented in Appendix 1 as reference.

10. This item means all costs of development of new products or services including software expenses and amortization of software costs. It excludes (1) customer or government-sponsored R & D, (2) extractive industry activities, such as prospecting, acquisition of mineral rights, drilling, mining etc., (3) engineering expense - routine ongoing efforts to define, enrich, or improve the qualities of existing products, (4) inventor royalties, and (5) market research and testing (Compustat Manual, 4/15/1986, Section 8, p. 80).

11. The data of fixed assests is obtained from the Compustat tapes, which is the item of property, plant and equipment - total (net).

12. Cash flow is defined as operating income before depreciation less interest payments and income taxes.

13.After we tried several different functional forms like log-log form, semi-log form, and differential form, we found that the simple linear model was the most suitable one. We obtained very low F-statistic and t-ratios for the explanatory variables from those models.

14. When we use the additive sum of subsequent years' data as a dependent variable, the model will be $FI_t + FI_{t-1} = f (VI_{t-1}, VI_{t-2}, VI_{t-3})$. As VI_{t-3} does not explain FI_t and VI_{t-1} does not explain FI_{t-1}, this model does not fit the causal relationship between dependent and independent variables.

Thus we estimated $FI_t + FI_{t-1} = f (VI_{t-2})$ and $FI_t + FI_{t-1} + FI_{t-2} = f (VI_{t-3})$, and we found that the results were not particularly different from those of $FI_t = f (VI_{t-1} + VI_{t-2})$ and $FI_t = f (VI_{t-1} + VI_{t-2} + VI_{t-3})$.

15. See Johnston, 1984, pp. 405-406.

16. Hall, Griliches and Hausman (1983, 1984) estimated nonlinear least squares model, Poisson model, and negative binomial model to deal with unobserved firm-specific effects (mainly size effects) without introducing firm dummy variables. Following them, under the assumption that the patents variable has a Poisson distribution where the disturbance is equal to the expected value, we estimated Poisson model by using Iterative Weighted Linear Least Squares estimation method. We found that the estimation results were not significantly different from the ones of OLS model.

17. See Judge et al., 1985, pp. 484-485.

18. When Hall, Griliches, and Hausman (1984) regressed five or seven lagged R & D variables on applied patents data, they got a negative sign on the first lagged R & D.

19. Armour and Teece (1980) refers FS^2 and FS^3 to the presence and relative importance of any economies or diseconomies of scale in R & D (p. 472).

20. R&D's minimum value is .2317, maximum value is 129.4641, and ranges from average .42 of the smallest firm to 69.14 of the largest firm.

21. This is fairly unexpected because the correlation coefficient between RND and sales (FS) is very small (-.1118).

22. We have seen from the empirical results that vertical integration at time t is affected by the innovative output of R&D and RND at time t and time t + 1. Finally, we construct

the model which includes the expectation variable as the form of $E_t(RND_t + RND_{t+1})$ on the right-hand-side of the VI_t equation, because it is theoretically assumed that both RND_t and RND_{t+1} affect VI_t at the same time. Unfortunately this model could not be solved without the help of the rational expectations hypothesis. But applying the methods of the rational expectations hypothesis did not allow the model to converge under the actual limitations of time and financial resources. The model is presented as an example in Appendix 2.

V
CONCLUSION

The purpose of this study was to investigate the relationship between a firm's decision to integrate vertically and its research and development strategy. This new dimension on the determinants of vertical integration has been explored both theoretically and empirically.

The theoretic background of our hypothesis centered on the "knowledge complementarity effect" of vertical integration and the "transaction costs" of technology trading. The knowledge complementarity effect was explained to be a mechanism through which vertical integration positively affects technological innovation. The transaction costs were the underlying reason for a firm's choice of internal R & D over using external technology market when the firm expects its future innovation to be significant.

The empirical work has been done in two steps. Firstly, to see if technologically vertical integration affects innovation, knowledge production functions were estimated through patents, R & D expenditure, and R & D intensity. Secondly, on the basis of this finding, the vertical integration equation was estimated in the dynamic simultaneous equation model to test the hypothesis that expected future innovation is an important determinant of vertical integration. Generally, the empirical results were supportive of our hypotheses.

This study has some important advantages as compared to previous studies of vertical integration and innovation. First, in analyzing the determinants of vertical integration, the externality effect of vertical integration and its relevant transaction costs were explained extensively. Second, it has tried to explain other firm-specific characteristics than firm size as the determinants of innovative output. Third, several different variables for innovative output such as patents, R & D expenditure, and R & D intensity were used. Fourth, it has explained the innovational aspect as an important determinant of vertical integration. Fifth, in order to explain this aspect an expectation variable was included as an explanatory variable for vertical integration. Sixth, this paper has employed a two-equation approach in order to investigate the main hypothesis directly from the behavioral equation and has employed a dynamic simultaneous equation method in order to be econometrically correct.

106

BIBLIOGRAPHY

Adelman, M. A., "Concept of Statistical Measurement of Vertical Integration," in G. J. Stigler (ed.), *Business Concentration and Public Policy* (Princeton:Princeton University Press, 1955).

Akerlof, G. A., "The Market for 'Lemons': Quality Uncertainty and the Market Mechanism," *Quarterly Journal of Economics* 84 (August 1970), 488-500.

Alchian, A. A. and H. Demsetz, "Production, Information Costs, and Economic Organization," *American Economic Review* 62 (December 1972), 777-795.

Allen, B. T., "Vertical Integration and Market Foreclosure: The Case for Cement and Concrete," *Journal of Law and Economics* 14 (April 1971), 251-274.

Anderson, E. and D. C. Schmittlein, "Integration of Sales Force: An Empirical Examination," *Rand Journal of Economics* 15 (Autumn 1984), 385-395.

Armour, H. O. and D. J. Teece, "Vertical Integration and Technological Innovation," *Review of Economics and Statistics* 62 (August 1980), 470- 474.

Arrow, K . J., "Economic Welfare and the Allocation of Resources for Invention," in *The Rate and Direction of Inventive Activity* (Princeton: Princeton University Press, 1962), 609-625.

---------- , "The Organization of Economic Activity," in Haveman, R. H. and J. Margolis (eds.), *Public Expenditure and Policy Analysis* (Chicago: Markham Publishing Co., 1971).

---------- , "Vertical Integration and Communication," *Bell Journal of Economics* 6 (Spring 1975), 173-183.

Arrow, K. J. and F. H. Hahn, *General Competitive Analysis* (San Francisco: Holden-Day Inc., 1971).

Bain, J. S., *Industrial Organization* (New York: John Wiley & Sons, Inc., 1959).

Bard, Yonathan, *Nonlinear Parameter Estimation* (Orlando: Academic Press, 1974).

Bernhardt, I., "Vertical Integration and Demand Variability," *Journal of Industrial Economics* 25 (March 1977), 213-229.

Blair, R. D. and D. L. Kaserman, *Law and Economics of Vertical Integration and Control* (New York: Academic Press, Inc., 1983).

Bound, John, Clint Cummins, Zvi Griliches, Bronwyn H. Hall, and Adam Jaffe, "Who does R & D and Who Patents?" in Zvi Griliches (ed.), *R & D, Patents, and Productivity* (Chicago: The University of Chicago Press, 1984), 21-53.

Carlton, D. W., "Vertical Integration in Competitive Markets under Uncertainty," *Journal of Industrial Economics* 27 (March 1979), 189-209.

Chandler, A. D., *Strategy and Structure* (New York: Doubleday & Co., 1966).

Coase, R. H., "The Nature of the Firm," *Economica* 4 (November 1937), 386-405.

Crandall, R. W., "Vertical Integration and the Market for Repair Parts in the U.S. Automobile Industry," *Journal of Industrial Economics* 16 (July 1968), 212-236.

Cremeans, John, Gurmukh Gill, Virgil Ketterling, Ann Lawson, and Kan Young, "Structural Change in the U.S. Economy: 1979-1987 High Technology versus Smokestack Industries," in U.S. Department of Commerce, *U.S. Industrial Outlook* (1984), 39-45.

Crocker, K. J., *Essays on Firm Structure with Private Information*, unpublished Ph. D dissertation, Carnegie-Mellon University (1981).

---------- , "Vertical Integration and the Strategic Use of Private Information," *Bell Journal of Economics* 14 (Autumn 1983), 236-248.

Eckard, E. W., "A Note on the Empirical Measurement of Vertical Integration," *Journal of Industrial Economics* 28 (September 1979), 105-107.

Evans, David and Sanford Grossman, "Integration," in D. Evans (ed.), *Breaking Up Bell* (New York: North Holland Publishing Co., 1983), 95-126.

Feller, Irwin, "The Economics of Technological Change Filtered Through a Social Knowledge System Framework," *Knowledge: Creation, Diffusion, Utilization* 9 (December 1987), 233-253.

Friar, John and Mel Horwitch, "The Emergence of Technology Strategy," *Technology in Society* 7 (1985), 143-178.

Friedman, M. N., "The Research and Development Factor in Mergers and Acquisitions," Study no. 16, U.S. Congress, Senate, Committee on the Judiciary, Subcommittee on Patents, Trademarks and Copyrights, 85th Cong., 2nd sess., 1958.

Gort, Michael, *Diversification and Integration in American Industry* (Princeton: Princeton University Press, 1962).

Griliches, Zvi, "Issues in Assessing the Contribution of Research and Development to Productivity Growth," *Bell Journal of Economics* 10 (Spring 1979), 92-116.

Hall, B. H., Zvi Griliches and J. A. Hausman, "Patents and R & D: Searching for a Lag Structure," NBER Working Paper No. 1227, 1983.

---------- , "Is There a Lag?" NBER Working Paper No. 1454, 1984.

Hippel, Eric von, "Cooperation between Rivals: Informal Know-how Trading," *Research Policy* 16 (1987), 291-302.

Jaffe, A. B., "Technological Opportunity and Spill-overs of R & D: Evidence from Firms' Patents, Profits and Market Value," *American Economic Review* 76 (December 1986), 984-1001.

Johnston, John, *Econometric Methods* (New York: McGraw-Hill, 1984).

Judge, G., R. Hill, W. Griffiths, H. Lutkepohl and T. Lee, *The Theory and Practice of Econometrics* (New York: John Wiley & Sons, Inc., 1985).

Kamien, M. I. and N. L. Schwartz, *Market Structure and Innovation* (New York: Cambridge University Press, 1982).

Klein, B., R. G. Crawford and A. A. Alchian, "Vertical Integration, Appropriable Rents and the Competitive Contracting Process," *Journal of Law and Economics* 21 (October 1978), 297-326.

Kline, S. J. and Nathan Rosenberg, "An Overview of Innovation," in Landau and Rosenberg (eds.), *The Positive Sum Strategy* (Washington, D. C.: National Academy Press, 1986), 275-305.

Kmenta, Jan, *Elements of Econometrics* (New York: Macmillan, 1971).

Kuznets, Simon, "Inventive Activity: Problems of Definition and Measurement," in *The Rate and Direction of Inventive Activity* (Princeton: Princeton University Press, 1962), 19-51.

Leibenstein, Harvey, "A Branch of Economics is Missing: Micro-Micro Theory," *Journal of Economic Literature* 17 (June 1979), 477-502.

Levy, D. T., *The Transactions Cost Approach to Vertical Integration: An Empirical Examination*, unpublished Ph.D dissertation, U.C.L.A. (1981).

---------- , "The Transactions Cost Approach to Vertical Integration: An Empirical Examination," *Review of Economics and Statistics* 67 (August 1985), 438-445.

MacDonald, J. M., "Market Exchange or Vertical Integration: An Empirical Analysis," *Review of Economics and Statistics* 67 (May 1985), 327-331.

McCallum, B. T., "Rational Expectations and the Natural Rate Hypothesis: Some Consistent Estimates," *Econometrica* 44 (January 1976), 43-52.

Machlup, Fritz, *Knowledge: Its Creation, Distribution, and Economic Significance* Vol. 1-3 (Princeton: Princeton University Press, 1980).

Mansfield, Edwin, "How Rapidly does New Industrial Technology Leak Out?" *Journal of Industrial Economics* 34 (December 1985), 217-223.

Masten, S. E., *Transaction Costs, Institutional Choice and the Theory of the Firm*, unpublished Ph.D dissertation, University of Pennsylvania (1982).

---------- , "The Organization of Production: Evidence from the Aerospace Industry," *Journal of Law and Economics* 27 (October 1984), 403-417.

---------- , "The Institutional Basis for the Firm," University of Michigan Working Paper, 1986, *Journal of Law, Economics and Organization*, Forthcoming.

Monteverde, Kirk and D. J. Teece, "Supplier Switching Costs and Vertical Integration in the Automobile Industry," *Bell Journal of Economics* 13 (Spring 1982), 206-213.

Mowery, D. C., "The Relationship between Intrafirm and Contractual Forms of Industrial Research in American Manufacturing, 1900-1940," *Explorations in Economic History* 20 (October 1983), 351-374.

National Science Board, *Science Indicators* 1985.

Nelder, J. A. and R. W. M. Wedderburn, "Generalized Linear Models," *J. R. Statist. Soc. A* (1972), 370-384.

Nelson, Richard R., "Institutions Supporting Technical Advance in Industry," *American Economic Review* 70 (May 1986), 186-189.

---------- , M. J. Peck and E. D. Kalachek, *Technology, Economic Growth and Public Policy* (Washington: Brookings Institution, 1967).

Obilichetti, B. R., *Backward Integration as a Strategic Decision: a Study of Captive Semi-conductor Production by a Minicomputer Manufacturer*, unpublished D.B.A. dissertation, Harvard University (1982).

Obstfeld, M., R. Cumby and J. Huizinga, "Two-Step, Two-Stage Least Squares Estimation in Models with Rational Expectations," NBER Technical Paper No. 11, 1981.

Pakes, Ariel and Zvi Griliches, "Patents and R & D at the Firm Level: A First Look," in Zvi Griliches (ed.), *R & D, Patents, and Productivity* (Chicago: The University of Chicago Press, 1984), 55-72.

Pennings, J. M., D. C. Hambrick and I. C. MacMillan, "Interorganizational Dependence and Forward Integration," *Organization Studies* 5/4 (1984), 307-326.

Perry, M. K., "Forward Integration by Alcoa: 1888-1930," *Journal of Industrial Economics* 29 (September 1980), 37-53.

Radner, Roy, "The Internal Economy of Large Firms," *The Economic Journal* 96 Supplement (1985), 1-22.

Ravenscraft, David J. and F. M. Scherer, *Mergers, Sell-Offs, and Economic Efficiency* (Washington: Brookings Institution, 1987).

Rothschild, Michael and Joseph Stiglitz, "Equilibrium in Competitive Insurance Markets," *Quarterly Journal of Economics* 80 (November 1976), 629-649.

Sanders, Barkev S., "Some Difficulties in Measuring Inventive Activity," in *The Rate and Direction of Inventive Activity* (Princeton: Princeton University Press, 1962), 53-90.

Sargent, T. J., *Macroeconomic Theory* (Orlando: Academic Press, Inc., 1979).

Scherer, F. M., *Industrial Market Structure and Economic Performance*, 2nd. ed. (Chicago: Rand McNally, 1980).

---------- , "Demand-Pull and Technological Invention: Schmookler Revisited," *Journal of Industrial Economics* 30 (March 1982), 225-237.

Schmookler, Jacob, *Invention and Economic Growth* (Cambridge: Harvard University Press, 1966).

Simon, Herbert A., *Administrative Behaviour* 2d ed. (New York: Macmillan Company, 1961).

Singer, Eugene M., *Antitrust Economics: Selected Legal Cases and Economic Models* (Englewood Cliffs, N. J.: Prentice Hall, 1968).

Taylor, J. B., "Estimation and Control of a Macroeconomic Model with Rational Expectations," *Econometrica* 47 (September, 1979), 1267-1286.

Teece, D. J., "Economies of Scope and the Scope of the Enterprise," *Journal of Economic Behavior and Organization* 1 (September 1980), 223-247.

---------- , "Profiting from Technological Innovation," *Research Policy* 15 (1986), 285-305.

---------- , "Capturing Value from Technological Innovation," in Guile and Brooks (eds.), *Technology and Global Industry* (Washington, D. C.: National Academy Press, 1987), 65-95.

Tucker, I. B. and R. P. Wilder, "Trends in Vertical Integration in the U.S. Manufacturing Sector," *Journal of Industrial Economics* 26 (September 1977), 81-94.

Vernon, J. M. and D. A. Graham, "Profitability of Monopolization by Vertical Integration," *Journal of Political Economy* 79 (July 1971), 924-925.

Wallis, K., "Econometric Implications of the Rational Expectations Hypothesis," *Econometrica* 48 (January, 1980), 49-74.

Warren-Boulton, F. R., "Vertical Control with Variable Proportions," *Journal of Political Economy* 75 (July 1974), 783-802.

---------- , *Vertical Control of Markets* (Cambridge: Ballinger Publishing Co., 1978).

Waterson, Michael, *Economic Theory of the Industry* (New York: Cambridge University Press, 1984).

Williamson, O. E. "The Vertical Integration of Production: Market Failure Considerations," *American Economic Review* 61 (May 1971), 112-123.

---------- , "Markets and Hierarchies: Some Elementary Considerations," *American Economic Review* 63 (May 1973), 316-325.

---------- , *Markets and Hierarchies: Analysis and Antitrust Implications* (New York: The Free Press, 1975).

---------- , *The Economic Institutions of Capitalism* (New York: The Free Press, 1985).

Appendix A
THE DISTRIBUTION OF PATENTS APPLIED FOR BY DATE GRANTED: 1970-1977

Year of Application	0	1	2	3	4	5+
			Years later			
1969	0	11	66	20	2	1
1970	0	18	62	17	2	1
1971	0	18	64	16	1	1
1972	0	30	60	8	1	1
1973	1	43	47	7	1	1
1974	2	48	43	5	1	1
1975	2	49	41	6	1	1
1976e	3	46	42	5	*	*
1977e	1	41	37	*	*	*

Based on a sample of 100,000 patents from the 1969-79 OTAF (Office of Technology Assessment and Forecasting at the NBER) tape on patents granted.

* not computable

e estimated

Source: Hall, Griliches, and Hausman (1983, Appendix)

Appendix B
ESTIMATING VI EQUATION WITH ADDITIVE SUM OF VARIABLE FI

The model is the two equations of

(1) $VI_t = a_1 VI_{t-1} + a_2 E_t(RND_t + RND_{t+1}) + a_3 CAP_t$

$\qquad + a_4 FS_t + a_5 CASH_t + a_6 VAR_t + a_7 TD + a_8 FD + u_t$

and

(2) $RND_t = b_1 RND_{t-1} + b_2 (VI_t + VI_{t-1}) + b_3 CAP_t + b_4 FS_t$

$\qquad + b_5 CASH_t + b_6 TD + b_7 FD + \eta_t$

where u_t and η_t are disturbances with mean zero, TD and FD are the vectors of year and time dummy variables, and a_7, a_8, b_6, and b_7 are the vectors of their parameters.

This is a dynamic simultaneous equation model with two added expectation variables and lagged variables. This model has the same problems with the previous ones. Although $E_t(RND_t) = RND_t$ since we assume that all the current variables are observable, $E_t(RND_{t+1})$ is unobservable. And $E_t(RND_t + RND_{t+1})$ is correlated with the disturbance term u_t. One thing different from the previous model is that an independent variable VI_t in equation (2) is correlated with the error term η_t. Therefore, equation (2) cannot be estimated by OLS.

To solve all the problems in estimating this model

we adopt the econometric technique used in the rational expectation studies of macroeconomics. At first we substitute (1) into (2) and get

(3) $RND_t = b_1 RND_{t-1} + b_2 \{ a_1 VI_{t-1} + a_2 E_t(RND_t)$

$\qquad + a_2 E_t(RND_{t+1}) + a_3 CAP_t + a_4 FS_t + a_5 CASH_t$

$\qquad + a_6 VAR_t + a_7 TD + a_8 FD + u_t + VI_{t-1} \} + b_3 CAP_t$

$\qquad + b_4 FS_t + b_5 CASH_t + b_6 TD + b_7 FD + \eta_t$

If we take expectations on both sides against information available at time t which is I_t, assuming $E_t \{ (b_2 u_t + \eta_t) \mid I_t \} = 0$, gives

(4) $(1 - b_2 a_2) E_t(RND_t) - b_2 a_2 E_t(RND_{t+1}) = E_t \{ b_1 RND_{t-1}$

$\qquad + (b_2 + b_2 a_1) VI_{t-1} + (b_3 + b_2 a_3) CAP_t + (b_4$

$\qquad + b_2 a_4) FS_t + (b_5 + b_2 a_5) CASH_t + b_2 a_6 VAR_t$

$\qquad + (b_6 + b_2 a_7) TD + (b_7 + b_2 a_8) FD \}$

Dividing both sides with $-1 / (b_2 a_2)$ gives

(5) $[1 - \{(1 - b_2 a_2) / (b_2 a_2)\} B] E_t(RND_{t+1}) = -1 / (b_2 a_2) E_t$

$\qquad$ [r.h.s.]

where B is a lag indicator. This can be rewritten as

(6) $(1 - \lambda B) E_t(RND_{t+1}) = -1 / (b_2 a_2) E_t$ [r.h.s.]

where $\lambda = (1 - b_2 a_2) / (b_2 a_2)$.
Assuming $|\lambda| < 1$,
$1 / (1 - \lambda B) = 1 + \lambda B + \lambda^2 B^2 + \lambda^3 B^3 + \cdots$.
Therefore, we get

(7) $E_t(RND_{t+1}) = [\{ 1 / (1 - \lambda B) \} \{ - 1 / (b_2 a_2) \}] E_t[r.h.s.]$

$= - \{ b_1 / (b_2 a_2) \} \Sigma_{i=0}^{\infty} \lambda^i E_t(RND_{t-1-i}) - \{ (b_2$

$+ b_2 a_1) / (b_2 a_2) \} \Sigma_{i=0}^{\infty} \lambda^i E_t(VI_{t-1-i}) - \{ (b_3 + b_2 a_3)$

$/ (b_2 a_2) \} \Sigma_{i=0}^{\infty} \lambda^i E_t(CAP_{t-i}) - \{ (b_4 + b_2 a_4)$

$/ (b_2 a_2) \} \Sigma_{i=0}^{\infty} \lambda^i E_t(FS_{t-i}) - \{ (b_5 + b_2 a_5) / (b_2 a_2) \}$

$\Sigma_{i=0}^{\infty} \lambda^i E_t(CASH_{t-i}) - \{ (b_2 a_6) / (b_2 a_2) \} \Sigma_{i=0}^{\infty} \lambda^i$

$E_t(VAR_{t-i}) - \{ (b6 + b_2 a_7) / (b_2 a_2) \} \{ 1 / (1$

$- \lambda) \} TD - \{ (b_7 + b_2 a_8) / (b_2 a_2) \} \{ 1 / (1 - \lambda) \} FD$

While the number of time lags i of the predetermined variables are infinite theoretically, it is confined to being a small integer in practice. We assume i = 2 because the time span in our data is so small. Under the assumption that all the past and current values are observable at time t, all the above expectation variables are realized values. Thus with $i = 2$ and $\lambda = (1 - b_2 a_2) / (b_2 a_2)$, we get

(8) $E_t(RND_{t+1}) = - \{ b_1 / (b_2 a_2) \} RND_{t-1} - [\{ b_1 (1 - b_2 a_2) \}$

$/ (b_2 a_2)^2 \} RND_{t-2} - [\{ b_1 (1 - b_2 a_2)^2 \} / (b_2 a_2)^3]$

$$RND_{t-3} - \{ (b_2 + b_2a_1) / (b_2a_2) \} \, VI_{t-1} - [\{ (b_2$$

$$+ b_2a_1)(1 - b_2a_2) \} / (b_2a_2)^2] \, VI_{t-2} - [\{ (b_2$$

$$+ b_2a_1)(1 - b_2a_2)^2 \} / (b_2a_2)^3] \, VI_{t-3} - \{ (b_3 + b_2a_3)$$

$$/ (b_2a_2) \} \, CAP_t - [\{ (b_3 + b_2a_3) (1 - b_2a_2) \}$$

$$/ (b_2a_2)^2] \, CAP_{t-1} - [\{ (b_3 + b_2a_3)(1 - b_2a_2)^2 \}$$

$$/ (b_2a_2)^3] \, CAP_{t-2} - \{ (b_4 + b_2a_4) / (b_2a_2) \} \, FS_t$$

$$- [\{ (b_4 + b_2a_4)(1 - b_2a_2) \} / (b_2a_2)^2] \, FS_{t-1}$$

$$- [\{ (b_4 + b_2a_4)(1 - b_2a_2)^2 \} / (b_2a_2)^3] \, FS_{t-2}$$

$$- \{ (b_5 + b_2a_5) / (b_2a_2) \} \, CASH_t - [\{ (b_3$$

$$+ b_2a_3)(1 - b_2a_2) \} / (b_2a_2)^2] \, CASH_{t-1} - [\{ (b_5$$

$$+ b_2a_5) (1 - b_2a_2)^2 \} / (b_2a_2)^3] \, CASH_{t-2} - \{ (b_2a_6)$$

$$/ (b_2a_2) \} \, VAR_t - [\{ b_2a_6 (1 - b_2a_2) \} / (b_2a_2)^2]$$

$$VAR_{t-1} - [\{ b_2a_6 (1 - b_2a_2)^2 \} / (b_2a_2)^3] \, VAR_{t-2}$$

$$- \{ (b_6 + b_2a_7) / (2b_2a_2 - 1) \} \, TD - \{ (b_7 + b_2a_8)$$

$$/ (2b_2a_2 - 1) \} \, FD$$

If we substitute (8) into (1) and let $E_t(RND_t) = RND_t$, we get VI_t equation as the function of endogenous variable RND_t and all the other predetermined variables. Since this equation and equation (2) constitute a simultaneous equation system, we substitute each equation into the other to get the reduced form equations

$$(9) \quad RND_{t+1} = - \{ b_1 / (b_2a_2) \} \, RND_{t-2} - [\{ b_1 (1 - b_2a_2) \}$$

$/ (b_2 a_2)^2]$ RND_{t-3} - { $(b_2 + b_2 a_1) / (b_2 a_2)$ } VI_{t-2}

- [{ $(b_2 + b_2 a_1) (1 - b_2 a_2)$ } $/ (b_2 a_2)^2$] VI_{t-3} - { $(b_2 a_3)$

$/ (1 - b_2 a_2)$ } CAP_t - { $(b_3 + b_2 a_3) / (b_2 a_2)$ } CAP_{t-1}

- [{ $(b_3 + b_2 a_3)(1 - b_2 a_2)$ } $/ (b_2 a_2)^2$] CAP_{t-2}

- { $(b_2 a_4) / (1 - b_2 a_2)$ } FS_t - { $(b_4 + b_2 a_4) / (b_2 a_2)$ }

FS_{t-1} - [{ $(b_4 + b_2 a_4)(1 - b_2 a_2)$ } $/ (b_2 a_2)^2$] FS_{t-2}

- { $(b_2 a_5) / (1 - b_2 a_2)$ } $CASH_t$ - { $(b_5 + b_2 a_5)$

$/ (b_2 a_2)$ } $CASH_{t-1}$ - [{ $(b_3 + b_2 a_3)(1 - b_2 a_2)$ }

$/ (b_2 a_2)^2$] $CASH_{t-2}$ - { $(b_2 a_6) / (1 - b_2 a_2)$ } VAR_t

- { $(b_2 a_6) / (b_2 a_2)$ } VAR_{t-1} - [{ $b_2 a_6 (1 - b_2 a_2)$ }

$/ (b_2 a_2)^2$] VAR_{t-2} + [{ $(b_2 a_2 b_6 - b_6 - b_2 a_2 a_7)$

$/ (2 b_2 a_2 - 1)$ } { $1 / (1 - b_2 a_2)$ }] TD + [{ $(b_2 a_2 b_7$

- $b_7 - b_2 a_2 a_8) / (2 b_2 a_2 - 1)$ } { $1 / (1 - b_2 a_2)$ }] FD

and

(10) VI_t = - VI_{t-1} { $(1 + a_1) / (b_2 a_2)$ } VI_{t-2} - { $(1 + a_1 - b_2 a_2$

- $b_2 a_2 a_1) / (b_2 a_2)^2$ } VI_{t-3} - (b_1 / b_2) RND_{t-1} - { b_1

$/ (a_2 b_2^2)$ } RND_{t-2} - { $(b_1 - b_2 a_2 a_1) / (b_2^3 a_2^2)$ } RND_{t-3}

- { b_3 / b_2 + $(a_2 b_2 a_3) / (1 - b_2 a_2)$ } CAP_t - { $(b_3$

+ $b_2 a_3) / (b_2^2 a_2)$ } CAP_{t-1} - { $b_3 + b_2 a_3 - b_2^2 a_2 a_3$

$$- b_3 b_2 a_2) / (b_2{}^3 a_2{}^2) \} \ CAP_{t-2} - \{ b_4 / b_2 + (a_2 b_2 a_4)$$

$$/ (1 - b_2 a_2) \} \ FS_t - \{ (b_4 + b_2 a_4) / (b_2{}^2 a_2) \} \ FS_{t-1} - \{ (b_4$$

$$+ b_2 a_4 - b_2{}^2 a_2 a_4 - b_4 b_2 a_2) / (b_2{}^3 a_2{}^2) \} \ FS_{t-2} - \{ b_5 / b_2$$

$$+ (a_2 b_2 a_5) / (1 - b_2 a_2) \} \ CASH_t - \{ (b_5 + b_2 a_5)$$

$$/ (b_2{}^2 a_2) \} \ CASH_{t-1} - \{ (b_5 + b_2 a_5 - b_2{}^2 a_2 a_5 - b_5 b_2 a_2)$$

$$/ (b_2{}^3 a_2{}^2) \} \ CASH_{t-2} - \{ (a_2 b_2 a_6) / (1 - b_2 a_2) \} \ VAR_t$$

$$- \{ a_6 / (b_2 a_2) \} \ VAR_{t-1} - \{ (a_6 - a_6 b_2 a_2) / (b_2{}^2 a_2{}^2) \}$$

$$VAR_{t-2} + [\{ a_2 (b_2 a_2 b_6 - b_6 - b_2{}^2 a_2 a_7) \} / \{ (2 b_2 a_2$$

$$- 1) (1 - b_2 a_2) \} + a_7] \ TD + [\{ a_2 (b_2 a_2 b_7 - b_7$$

$$- b_2{}^2 a_2 a_8) \} / \{ (2 b_2 a_2 - 1) (1 - b_2 a_2) \} + a_8] \ FD$$

Both equations (9) and (10) are the reduced form equations with all the observable predetermined variables as explanatory variables. Since they did not have any simultaneity problem, we estimated equations (9) and (10) using the SYSNLIN OLS method. Unfortunately, demanding computer-related financial resources kept us short of getting the results. It is likely that the micro data, as compared to macro data (especially this kind of pooled time-series, cross-sectional data), does not produce good empirical results for the rational expectations model. As far as econometric aspects, this model does not appear to have any deficiencies.

Index

Adelman, M. A., 48-9, 54-6
Akerlof, G. A., 18, 33
Alchian and Demsetz, 28, 61
Alcoa, 8
Allen, B. T., 8
Anderson and Schmittlein, 9, 34, 47
Armour and Teece, 7, 21, 24, 42, 47, 54, 57, 62, 85, 102
Arrow, K. J., 9, 13, 27, 32
Arrow - Hahn, 28
asset specificity, 10, 31
asymmetric information problem, 31-7

backward integration, 55-60
Bain, J. S., 9
Ben Franklin Partnership Program, 22
Bernhardt, T., 9, 62-3
Blair and Kaserman, 10
bounded rationality, 10, 31

capital intensity, 60
Carlton, D. W., 9, 40
Chain-Linked Model, 25
Chandler, A. D., 9
Coase, R., 4, 9, 12, 28-9, 61
contract relationship, 30
Crandall, R. W., 8
Cremeans et. al., 18
Crocker, K. J., 14, 27, 33

Datamation, 40-1
diminishing returns to management, 9, 61
Dummy variable, 73-4
dynamic simultaneous equation model, 6, 43

Eckard, E. W., 48
employee shirking, 28, 61
employment relationship, 30
error component model, 72
externality effect, 5, 13, 28

Feller, Irwin, 21
forward integration, 49
Friar and Horwitch, 3
Friedman, M. N., 20
future innovation, 37, 42

Generalized Least Squares(GLS), 72
Gort, M., 48

Hall, Griliches and Hausman, 57, 59, 102
Hippel, E. V., 41
human capital, 15, 34

industry concentration, 48
information asymmetry problem, 6, 31
information impactedness, 11
informational economies, 6, 21
internalization cost, 11-5, 60

Johnston, J., 44, 102
Judge et al., 47, 102

Kamien and Schwartz, 61
Kline and Rosenberg, 25, 50
Kmenta, J., 44
knowledge complementarity effect, 5, 6, 15, 28
knowledge transfer, 28, 35

learning-by-doing, 32
Leibenstein, H., 41, 49
Levy, D. T., 9, 14, 49, 51, 54-5, 57, 61

MacDonald, J. M., 60
Machlup, F., 7, 23, 28, 32, 35
Maddala, G. S., 73
"make or buy" decision, 12-6
Mansfield, E., 36
Masten, S., 9, 13-4, 28-9, 38, 41, 47
Monteverde and Teece, 9, 13, 47
Mowery, D. C., 9, 34
Mundlak, 72

negative knowledge, 7
Nelson, R. R., 23

Obilichetti, B. R., 40
Ordinary Least Squares (OLS), 70

patents, 70
Pearson product-moment correlation matrix, 68
Pennings, Hambrick and MacMillan, 48
Perry, M.K., 8
PIMS, 48

R & D contracting, 11
R & D expenditure, 60
R & D intensity, 58
R & D spillover, 100
Radner, R., 41, 49
rational expectations hypothesis, 6
recursive model, 47, 90
Rothschild and Stiglitz, 18

Scherer, F. M., 7, 40, 59
Schmookler, J., 59
Schumpeterian hypothesis, 5
Simon, H. A., 29
Singer, E. M., 54
Standard and Poor's, 49
strategic business unit (SBU), 48
SYSNLIN OLS, 92-3

technological complementarity, 22
technological endowment, 54, 85
technology leakage, 37
technology licensing, 12
Teece, D. T., 30, 33, 35, 37, 61-2
thermal economies, 15
threshold effect, 98
transaction cost, 12-6
Tucker and Wilder, 48-9, 54-5, 57
two-stage least squares (2SLS), 47

Vernon and Graham, 9
vertical integration, 54, 59
vertical merger, 20

Warren-Boulton, 6, 9
Washington University, 22
Williamson, O. E., 4, 9-11, 21-2, 27-9, 31, 36, 41, 60

Printed in the United States
by Baker & Taylor Publisher Services